Stories of Survival

The People of Ferramonti: Then and Now

Yolanda Ropschitz-Bentham

Stories of Survival
The People of Ferramonti: Then and Now

by
©2021 Yolanda Ropschitz-Bentham

Published by Texianer Verlag
Tuningen
Germany

www.texianer.com

ISBN: 978-3-949197-81-9

All rights reserved

Front cover illustration:
Sephardic style menorah from Spain
By Roylindman at English Wikipedia, CC BY-SA 3.0, https://commons.wikimedia.org/w/index.php?curid=17960934

DEDICATION

**To the memory of my big brother Manfred Roxon-Ropschitz
(21.7 1950 – 7.11.2021)**

He did not suffer fools, gladly or otherwise.

We, his family, mourn his untimely passing.

ACKNOWLEDGEMENTS

I would like to thank

- All my contributors, in particular Avner Halevy, for their incredible patience. They wrote the stories, delved into family archives, contacted distant relatives, scanned photos and replied to an endless stream of emails from me. Without them, there would be no book.
- Simonetta Heger for her translation of the story of Sultana Razon Veronesi.
- Prof Mario Rende and Simona Celiberti for their knowledge of Ferramonti and dedication to preserving its memory.
- The very special man, Stephen Engelking, friend and publisher. The stories of Ferramonti have touched him; I hope they do the same for all who read them.

ABOUT THE AUTHOR

Born in Derby in 1953, Yolanda grew up in West Yorkshire, in the north of England, a region famed for its wild and barren heather-clad landscapes. Her home town was barely a stone's throw from the windy moors of Haworth, the home of the Bronte sisters. These bleak vistas etched in her a deep and enduring love of nature, heath and moorland.

With an extended family in mainland Europe, USA and Australasia and a multi-lingual father, the love of travel and learning new languages was instilled from an early age along with an enjoyment of amateur dramatics, writing and choral singing. After studying languages at school, then at college in Manchester followed by a stint as an au pair in Geneva, she travelled to Israel where she worked for three years in a multinational travel agency, firstly in Tel Aviv, then in London and Philadelphia.

In 1979 she returned to academic study, graduating with a BSc (Hons) in Psychology at the University of Bradford in 1982. This led to a period of two years working at the pioneering Caldecott Therapeutic Community in Kent.

In 1984 she relocated to Bristol where she met her husband. They settled in rural Somerset where they established a small holding, raising three children amid ducks, geese, chickens, sheep and apple orchards. It was not quite the Yorkshire moors but was often wild and windy!

In 1992 Yolanda began teaching Psychology, a career which was to span 25 years. In between teaching, raising her family and wild food foraging she turned to writing comic pieces, two of which were featured on BBC Somerset radio.

In recent years, Yolanda has worked as a volunteer presenter on local radio, interviewing guests and delivering her own contributions on a variety of topics.

Following retirement in 2016 Yolanda turned to her late father's manuscript, "Ferramonti." Researching his autobiographical novel over the next few years led to regular visits to the Ferrramonti di Tarsia camp museum in Calabria. Through these trips she was lucky and honoured to meet former internees from the 1940s and their descendants. This connection, culminating in the publication of her father's novel, "Ferramonti: Salvation behind the barbed wire", has produced one of the most rewarding periods of her life so far, affording Yolanda cherished opportunities to travel to Italy, Israel and South America. Life stories from former internees have now formed the heart of her second publication which you have before you: "Stories of Survival: The People of Ferramonti, Then and Now".

PREFACE

While editing my late father's book (Ferramonti: Salvation behind the barbed wire) I became so immersed in the life of this extraordinary *Campo di Concentramento* in Calabria that my interest did not end with the book's publication in 2020. Instead, it led me to seek out stories from other survivors who might want to share their experiences from those dark times. Some are tales of triumph, others are full of tragedy.

The population of Ferramonti was not static; from June 1940 to its closure in December 1945, internees were arriving and departing all the time. At its fullest, the camp housed around 3,000 internees. This means there are a great many stories still untold.

A few adverts placed on *JewishGen* resulted in the following accounts; they come from Israel, USA, South America and Europe, written by survivors or their relatives. I am honoured to share their recollections in this book; my role has simply been to edit and let the stories speak for themselves.

Yolanda Ropschitz-Bentham
Somerset, 2021

Contents

DEDICATION	3
ACKNOWLEDGEMENTS	5
ABOUT THE AUTHOR	7
PREFACE	9
Introduction	13
Miriam Aflalo	15
Samuel Avisar (Rewisorski)	21
Ed and Sultana Berger	25
Lisa (Lisl) and Henry Bernstein	35
Ruth Bernstein-Bieber	41
Maurizio Chotiner	47
Shlomo and Anna Danziger	51
Riccardo Ehrman	57
Isacco Friedmann	61
Albert Goldfield	67
Richard and Else Goldstein	73
Stefan Greiwer	77
Yehoshua and Shoshana Halevy	83
Kienwald Family	89
Zew Kutten	99
Ernesto and Anny Lazar	101
Siegfried and Hilda Margoniner	105
Richard and Hella Mayer	111
Zvi Neumann and Gita Friedmann	121
Moszek Paserman and Chana Cukier	133
Sami (Shalom) Prisant	141

Sultana Razon Veronesi	143
David Ropschitz	153
Amalia and Aron Schöps	161
Mordechai Schwartz	167
Yehuda Spiegel	175
Shlomo and Sara Zelmanovitch	179
Adolfo (Foffo) Zippel	183

Introduction

In Calabria, June 1940, Jewish exiles from Europe, escaping the Nazis, begin to arrive at Ferramonti di Tarsia Campo di Concentramento, a site chosen by the Fascist Italian government for its remoteness and inhospitable terrain. The aim: to intern 'enemy aliens' resident in Italy as the country enters WWII.

Over the next three years, Ferramonti will see its population swell to over 3,000 internees, mostly, but not all, Jews from central and eastern Europe. Large contingents arriving via Benghazi and the Danube paddle-steamer Pentcho, will settle in Ferramonti, making it their haven as the war rages and the Nazis commit their atrocities, decimating families left behind.

Little did those internees know that Ferramonti would become their salvation; the barbed wire surrounding the camp would form a protective ring around them. They lost their freedom but ultimately escaped with their lives, thanks to the humane treatment afforded by their Italian captors.

But Ferramonti had a shifting population; some arrived and remained till liberation in September 1943, some departed to other fates, sometimes worse. In this book, you can read the stories of some of those survivors: their lives before, during and after captivity in Italy's largest internment camp, Ferramonti di Tarsia.

Miriam Aflalo

My name is Miriam Aflalo, a native of Slovakia, the only daughter of Bella and Zvi Malinowski. My father immigrated to Eretz Israel in early September 1939 to get a job and a roof over his head. My mother and I were supposed to join him a few months later. Meanwhile, the war broke out and separated us. After hardships and wanderings we found ourselves in Ferramonti camp in southern Italy. I was five years old.

My memories of life in the camp left a mark on me with mixed feelings; sadness, fear, anxiety but also joy, moments of happiness, a feeling of a big and embracing family, protected by my mother and our Pentcho family.

Beyond the camp fence was a spectacular flower field. I loved standing there and happily gazing at the colourful flowers which I longed to pick and give to my mother. One day, bright and springy, I did a daring act and fearlessly passed the guards, who apparently did not notice me, and advanced towards the beautiful space in front of me. Reaching the edge of the field I felt my feet sink. Suddenly I could not move, I could no longer see the flowers, and all my attention was focused on what was happening to me—I was sinking and unable to lift a leg to walk. Today, in retrospect, it is clear to me that my reactive behaviour was the only option a person could choose when in danger—to freeze. Without being able to escape the danger or fight it, I froze physically and mentally. I do not remember how long I froze there in that spot, but at a certain moment a horse appeared in the distance. I did not shout, I was paralysed with terror, but I saw him enter with his horse into the swamp. He approached me and pulled me out. My shoes were left abandoned in the scary mud, and the rider sat me on his horse, sat down behind me and so we entered the camp. Fear thawed and as in fairy tales—so I felt—the princess returned to the palace. I did not bring flowers to my mother, but I will not forget this story for the rest of my life.

In the last months of the war we noticed planes, which emerged from somewhere and bombed the area where the camp was located. Whenever we heard the noise of the planes, my mother urged me to lie down and she joined me. We both lay there hugging, until the noise subsided and we came out of hiding and stood on our feet. One such day I especially remember. A bomb fell in the camp and I found myself walking with my mother, holding hands, as if in a hurry or running away, and along the narrow pathway people flocked in the same direction. It was quiet. No one made a sound. After the noise of the planes, the silence intensified even more. As a child who did not understand what was going on, it was a surreal and unimaginable sight. As we continued we saw more and more people, camp refugees, in a hurry and almost running. We stopped only when we reached a large crowd of people surrounding the square at the end of the pathway. There I saw a corpse lying on the ground and its stomach open. Here, too, as in the swamp, I fell silent, as if I had disconnected from all my emotions. I could not move; I was frozen to the spot. My mother later told me that the victim was the camp watchmaker. When the engines of the planes began to sound, he decided not to hide, and as if in defiance, he went out into the street for fresh air. His wife's pleas did not help. The result of the attack was the watchmaker was killed and the work area where he would repair the clocks was destroyed.

One day, after the liberation of the camp, we went out with some friends to play. We chose the wide sandy path which led outside the camp limits. Suddenly a military car appeared and stopped in front of us across the path. A uniformed soldier got out of the vehicle, all smiling, and with a hand gesture asked us to cross the path and access it. We were filled with apprehension. We did not move. The soldier took a camera out of his pocket and signalled to us that he wanted to take our picture. We still did not dare to approach. He asked, pleaded, reached out and kept smiling. Hesitantly, but determined, I crossed the path and approached him. He sat down on a mound, invited me to approach and sit on his knee. Meanwhile, another soldier got out of the military vehicle, took the camera in his hands and photographed me sitting on the first soldier's knee. My friends refused to be photographed.

At the end of the war I was given the photo at one of the Pentcho gatherings we had in the lobby of a hotel, where I met the anonymous soldier who introduced himself to me: David Bromberger by name. He moved me greatly and surprised me when he handed me the photo. The picture, which he gave me when it was enlarged, stands on my desk to this day.

Daily life in Ferramonti

I lived with my mother in one "apartment" with another family. The residence was a one-story wooden building with several rooms. Perla, a girl two years younger than me, was the only daughter of the family with us; we played in the afternoon. Before lunch you were busy studying. Yes, I was in first grade where I learned to write Latin letters, and maybe a few words in German, which was my mother tongue. Twice a week, as far as I can remember, I studied ballet. I have a picture, where I am in ballet costume standing with outstretched hands and showing off my white dress.

In the centre of the camp was a bakery; a round structure with a large round oven. There we brought, every Friday, the pot containing *khomin*, made from dried beans and rice. In general, most of the food we ate in the camp was rice and cabbage. I have a photo where my mother and I are drinking soup on a cold winter's day.

My mother used to sit for many hours at the table, in the room, playing patience. She was a quiet and pleasant woman, respectful. A good, protective mother. You felt confident. She always used to tie a white ribbon in my hair and dress me in a clean dress and polished shoes. She passed away at the age of 86 and I still have questions I did not ask her. For example, where did the dresses, shoes and shoe polish come from; or how she felt as a lonely woman whose husband was not there in the difficult situations of *aliyah*? My father emigrated to Eretz Israel before the outbreak of the war, to prepare accommodation and work for our arrival. The war separated us for over four years, until we arrived in Israel and then I met him for the first time since I was two years old.

In the Land of Israel

At the end of the war, when I was seven, my mother and I boarded the ship, *Stefano*. We were all excited and happy to finally be on our way to the Land of Israel. The first stop was Alexandria, Egypt. There we boarded a train that took us north to Atlit. From the train window, I saw a camel for the first time. I was surprised to see such a strange animal, and whenever I see a camel I am reminded of this "historic" drive. In Atlit, I first met my father, who came to take us to our new home in the city of Petah Tikva. He knew about our arrival through the Red Cross.

The new "house" was one room without a kitchen, bathroom, or toilet; these were in a neglected yard we shared with our neighbours. A kind of Ferramonti—in the Land of Israel. Petah Tikva is a city in the centre of the country and the meaning of its name does indeed express everything we went through during the four years of the war on our long journey to the homeland— *Tikva* (Hope).

In Petah Tikva, I started attending an organized school. I did not know Hebrew. I had a hard time communicating with the kids and with the teacher. But it was not long before I adapted to the new life. I started speaking the local language, playing with the children in the schoolyard, and reading books. The first book I understood from the beginning to the end made me happy and joyful. A few years ago I looked for it at a well-known book collector but the book was not found. Ferramonti was far behind. Only the memories remain.

My father, a construction worker, was hardworking, and loved to laugh. My mother was a housewife, maybe frustrated, maybe disappointed. It took her a long time until she learned to speak basic Hebrew, but was unable to pursue the profession she had in Slovakia, working in a travel agency.

We lived in Petah Tikva for one year. From there we moved to a new settlement called Givat Shmuel. Here I felt like inside a palace; three rooms + bathroom + kitchen + large yard. I got lost and I was happy. My father—with an Arab labourer—

turned the yard into a beautiful and flourishing garden. In the yard, we raised chickens and ducks. A pear tree bore large, juicy fruit and even a dog ran about wagging its tail happily.

Givat Shmuel offered a good and satisfying life. The settlement developed quickly; roads were paved, an avenue of trees was opened and between them green benches, there was a delivery of milk to houses and also blocks of ice to cool the food. They set up a small school on a hill, close to our house, where I studied until the age of 14.

I went to study at a high school (Gymnasium) in the city of Ramat Gan, a twenty-minute drive from Givat Shmuel. Upon graduation from the Gymnasium, at eighteenth grade, I studied for two years at a teachers' seminary, and after receiving a teaching certificate I enlisted in the army, to work as a soldier-teacher in the south of the country, in the Negev, a two-hour drive from where I lived. Working in the Negev, in an agricultural community, in a small school, was the most beautiful placement of my life: "teacher Miriam."

Two years later, I returned to my parents' house and continued to work as a teacher in the centre of the country. At the age of twenty-four, I had three sons, and today I have nine grandchildren and one great-grandchild.

In the meantime, I also managed to study at the Adler Institute, which prepares students to lead parent groups on the subject of "good parenting" according to Adlerian theory. I also studied at the institute, which trained students to be family counsellors; it was a beautiful and interesting period of my life.

I still have a good relationship with one of the survivors of the Pentcho group. It is important for me to mention his name —Haim Farkash—because he is the one who initiated exciting meetings with all our immigrant friends, a roots trip along our entire success route through Israel, and also the erection of a monument to our ship, Pentcho, in a large square in Netanya.

And to pass on the story of our *aliyah* to future generations, I tell it every year to groups of teenagers as well as adults, on the eve of Holocaust Remembrance Day.

Miriam Aflalo, Israel

Miriam

Miriam with David Bromberger

Samuel Avisar (Rewisorski)

My father Samuel of blessed memory was born in Frankfurt am Main, Germany, in December 1913 to the Rewisorski family who emigrated from Poland around the year 1905.

After his father's death when he was just seven years old, my father was transferred to an orphan home in Frankfurt, where he grew up and was educated an Orthodox Jewish education, following the way of Rabbi Shimshon Rafael Hirsch.

In the year 1933, when he graduated high school as an outstanding pupil, he joined a group of young people who intended to establish a Yeshiva in the community of Fiume, near Trieste, in Fascist Italy's north east. The head of the Yeshiva was Rabbi Joseph Breuer.

In 1938, following Kristallnacht, the Yeshiva was closed down and Rabbi Breuer emigrated to the United States. My father decided to remain in Italy; he moved to Venice and registered in the Faculty of Linguistics at the University. But in the summer of 1940 he was detained due to being Jewish with foreign citizenship (in fact, he was stateless and was carrying a Nansen passport). He was sent to Ferramonti di Tarsia, alone and separated from all his friends.

My father remained in Ferramonti for about four years. After the liberation of the camp by the Allied forces in September 1943, he made the decision to move to Israel the following year.

I will try to describe life in Ferramonti from the few stories he told me during my childhood. I will also draw on parts from Carlo Spartaco Capogreco's book, "Ferramonti," (Giuntina 1987). In this book there are several quotes that my father, Samuel Avisar, wrote at the request of Fondo Israele Kalk in Milan, about his memories from Ferramonti camp.

He told me that a special hut for observant Jews was erected in the camp. Naturally, being an orthodox Jew, my father was one of the initiators of this construction.

One of the challenging missions in camp life was to prepare Kosher food for the internees. My father was nominated to be the "Economist"... his duty was to calculate, plan and order food products that were suitable for keepers of Kashrut, out of the poor supply they had, and together with the 'cook' they took care to prepare purely Kosher meals in the kitchen that was common to all inmates of their dwelling. I remember as an adult trying to calculate the quantities required for a large 'seven blessings' meal. My father said, "What's the problem? You need to calculate pasta by so-and-so grams per person..." He had not forgotten the skills he acquired by the force of his duty in Ferramonti!

Also, prayers in *Minyan* (ten people) were held in the 'religious' barrack and they built a synagogue as well. Also, Jewish holidays were celebrated according to all the traditional details, as best as they could. In this area too, my father was very active.

A few times, my father mentioned Rabbi Riccardo Pacifici, the chief Rabbi of Genoa, whom everybody applied to with any questions and requests, and he always made great efforts to help Ferramonti's internees, visiting the camp on numerous occasions. He performed several weddings in Ferramonti and made a rule that a bride could take her pre-marital purifying plunge in the local river, as there was no *Mikveh* in the camp. Following this, it was necessary to achieve permission from the police chief at that time, Maresciallo Marrari, to perform this ceremony outside the perimeter fence. According to witnesses, he was a good-hearted man who did his best to improve the detainees' conditions, and so he co-operated.

The internees established a school in Ferramonti for all the children to learn reading and writing, mathematics and literature. It was also a place where the children (some of them lonely and without parents) found an identity. After Ferramonti and until his last breath, my father's principal goal in life was education just as in Ferramonti where he was teaching Jewish children in various matters.

As is known, refugees from the Pentcho Ma'apilim ship (that sailed off from Bratislava in May 1940) reached Ferramonti in spring of 1942. These detainees made a major contribution to the camp's communal life. In his memoirs, my father describes how he got acquainted with Jews from Eastern Europe, who were so different in their habits, ways of life, their culture and their temperament from what he was used. And so, Ferramonti was a small-scale preparation for what he would encounter in the Land of Israel after his *aliyah*.

In retrospect:

These are the very few details and stories that I was lucky to hear directly from my father. Much to my great sorrow, he did not share much of his life story, for reasons that he kept to himself, and I did not know then how to ask and insist on receiving answers. His belief was that we should not dwell on the past but make the most of the present.

My feeling about Ferramonti is that despite all the challenges in the camp, not everything was black and negative. People survived, they got on with things and coped; there was no despair. There were positive aspects too in the creation of communal life. So different from other camps...

I thank God for the fact that my father got to Ferramonti, otherwise we would not be here. A positive feeling arises from parts of his memories quoted in Capogreco's book and also from the atmosphere I absorbed in my childhood.

After Ferramonti:

Some time after the liberation of the camp, my father moved to Israel, took part in the War of Independence and became a high school teacher.

A few years later he decided to return to Italy and complete his university studies for a doctorate in literature and linguistics. At the same time he was giving Hebrew and Judaism lessons to young people in Milan. In time, one of his students became his wife.

For about twenty years my father was a lecturer in Hebrew Language and Literature at the University of Strasbourg, France. In 1980 he returned to Israel for good, and settled in Jerusalem. He died in 1999 in Jerusalem.

May his Soul be bound in the Bond of Life

Varda Reiner, Israel

Ed and Sultana Berger

Ed Berger

He was born Srecko Berger on November 13, 1922, in Osijek, Yugoslavia, in what is now Croatia, the biggest city in its east and close to what is now the Serbian border. He came from a prosperous family, but his parents were divorced when he was 7. His mother, Margit Berger, returned to her hometown to live with her parents. His father, Edmund Berger, struggled to make a living, remarried and was living in Belgrade when the war broke out. Srecko lived with his grandmother in Osijek until she died, when he was 14. He left what was now his uncle's house at 16, going to Zagreb to finish high school, or gymnasium, and supporting himself as best he could.

The Germans invaded on April 6, 1941, and Croatia, pro-German, was occupied without resistance. The Germans established an independent Croatian fascist state. Fearing youths organizing against them, they closed the schools and my father was given his diploma. Jews were required to wear a Jewish star, kept out of restaurants and subjected to curfews. One good memory my father had of this period was a traditional graduation dinner at a restaurant with students and professors. He and other Jewish students decided to risk going, violating various restrictions, and removed their Jewish stars. What pleased him is that none of the other students, including the Croatians, informed on them. The evening went as planned.

A couple of months later the Germans posted a list of young men required to report for labour duty. My father's closest friend, Robert Abraham, whose family had fled Vienna around the Anschluss, was on the list. The young men on it were mostly from wealthy families. My father wasn't on it. He decided to go with Robert anyway, to get his labour duty over with and stay with his friend. But they wouldn't take him. Robert went and was never heard from again. My father heard later that he was thrown over a cliff by the Croatian Ustashe.

My father knew he had to leave Zagreb. His hometown of Osijek, far to the east, didn't seem safer. Meanwhile, defeated Yugoslav troops were being repatriated to their home regions. My father learned such a train was headed for Ljubljana, Slovenia, only an hour to the west; and Slovenia was occupied by Italy, not Germany. Srecko had a school friend, Miroslav Mrvos, a Serb, whose older sister supplied my father with false documentation getting him on the train. The day it left, in July 1941, he went to the station, with one of his friends carrying his suitcase so it wouldn't look like he himself was going anywhere. He slipped onto the train and got to Ljubljana without incident.

He lived in a Red Cross shelter there for a while. For a couple of months he worked as a farm labourer in the countryside, pretending to be Serbian Orthodox and sleeping in a barn. He had an uncle whom he met up with in Susak, what is now Rijeka on the Dalmatian coast. It was Croatian, and the local police targeted Jews, but also under Italian occupation. They returned to Ljubljana at some point. They were without proper documents, running out of money, and had both failed to report to the Croatian police in Susak after having been summoned. Ljubljana was also becoming risky. German lines were only five miles away, Tito's partisans were attacking to provoke them, and German retaliation might include occupying Ljubljana or rounding up Jews or both. The Jewish leaders suggested my dad and his uncle turn themselves in, to the Italians. They'd heard the Italians were treating Jews fairly. My dad and Uncle Ernest did so in Susak's Italian sister city, Fiume, in February 1942. They were given train tickets to travel to Ferramonti, as far from German lines as you could get in continental Europe. They travelled separately. Dad stopped twice, once to visit an aunt in Padua, and in Rome just to sightsee. (On a visit there with me in 2000 we were at the Piazza Repubblica. He pointed to a McDonald's there and said, "When I was here in 1942 that was a cafe and there were German officers sitting at it.") He was arrested the second time and put back on the train. He arrived at Ferramonti without further incident.

At Ferramonti he was placed in a barrack for single men, of which he at 19 was the youngest. He remembered a guard telling him early on, "In two years you will be the guards and we will be the prisoners." He believed the Italians' refusal to mistreat the Jewish inmates stemmed in part from their conviction that they were losing the war and that after North Africa fell to the Allies, Italy would be next. A key element was that the fascist detail sent by Rome to the camp wasn't allowed inside. It guarded outside the wire, but local civil administration from the Cosenza area ran the camp on the inside.

Food was scarce at Ferramonti. My father volunteered to work in the kitchen hoping to get more to eat but decided the additional calories he could get weren't worth the additional calories he expended working. Food was available on the black market — the guards and prisoners colluded on that — but he didn't have much money. He lost weight steadily in 1942. In a diary he kept during that period, he expressed fears that he would starve to death. He wrote to his family back in Yugoslavia, asking them to send him his best suit; he needed to sell it for money.

He established a study regimen for himself, each day an hour for each subject such as sciences, maths and languages. He had learned to play the guitar in Zagreb, sometimes rehearsing with jazz musicians, the Devil's Band, for which Robert Abraham had played piano. While he didn't have a guitar, he gave lessons at Ferramonti to a guy who did. When that man bought his release out of the camp — he accepted conversion to Catholicism and the Church helped him emigrate to South America — he gave my father his guitar. We still have it. At this moment of writing we are seeking to have it repaired.

Dad recalled that Uncle Ernest, 13 years his senior, was part of a group of men known as "the general staff". They sat around analysing the progress of the war, based on what news they could get, and tried to predict what would happen. The camp commandant had a Jewish girlfriend from among the prisoners, and she spent evenings with him. He listened, illegally of course, to the BBC. The girlfriend heard the news and passed it on to other inmates.

Food was scarce but medical care was good. The Italians followed the Geneva Conventions in their treatment of the prisoners. My father stressed this in his interview with the Spielberg project. The prisoners received preventive medicine for malaria, which was endemic in the area, and even local residents didn't always have it available.

Dad recalled the arrival in March 1942 of the passengers of the Danube riverboat Pentcho, who had set sail from Bratislava in May 1940 full of hopes of reaching Palestine. The Pentcho ran aground in the Aegean Sea; the passengers were all saved and sent to Rhodes where they remained in captivity for over a year under extreme conditions. Some of the young men were members of Betar, who had set off from Bratislava all that time ago with the intention of joining the Irgun. They seemed well organised and tough in their leather jackets. But all the passengers were united in their common goal of reaching the land of Israel. My father recalled that some of the passengers had manage to salvage, among other things, a store of medicines and pharmaceuticals.

Sultana Salomon Berger

My mother was born Sultana Salomon in Belgrade, March 1, 1923. Her father Moshe Salomon was in the import-export business, and her mother, Tilde Ferro Salomon, was from Corfu, Greece. Tilde's father had been the Jewish community president in Corfu and at least two ancestors had been rabbis of the Sephardic/Italian synagogue there.

Moshe and Tilde met during the First World War, when Moshe, a Serb Army officer and aide to a general, retreated with the Serbian Army south to the Adriatic Sea and then to Corfu. He was married at that time, but his wife died after the war. He later returned to propose to Tilde. They led a comfortable life, owning not one but two Steinway grand pianos, which were intended for my mother and her sister. The Germans looted them in 1941.

My mother went to a business high school where she received secretarial training in shorthand and typing, and won a shorthand competition. She supported the family after the war with her secretarial skills, first working for Allied naval intelligence in Palermo and later for the American Joint Jewish Distribution Committee in Rome. She was multi-lingual—not only Serbo-Croatian but Italian, German, French with smatterings of Ladino, Greek, Hebrew and English—making her a valuable employee who could talk to almost any refugee who showed up.

When the Germans attacked in April 1941 Belgrade was heavily bombed. My mother was at her married older sister's house during the bombing and it took a direct hit from a Stuka. They were in the basement. One resident was killed.

Moshe left on April 8, 1941, two days after the Germans attacked, when Yugoslavia was still resisting, with my mother's younger brother Nello, then 16. Moshe did not delude himself that things would improve. He feared the Germans and acted instantly when the war started. He reasoned two men could move faster than a large family unit, that he would move family money out of the country and that he would send back couriers and guides with documents to get the family out. He had been an officer in the First World War and the Balkan Wars, and had connections. He and Nello survived a harrowing journey to the coast. Their column was attacked by German fighter planes, and Nello would recall a soldier handing him a rifle so he could shoot back at the planes. At one point their hotel room was tossed by police searching for the gold they were sure the Jews had on them, but they didn't find it. It was hidden in a cigarette pack my grandfather set on the table in front of them, offering them a smoke.

Moshe and Nello went north to Split, held by the Italians, and sent for Tilde, Sulty, her older married sister Stella, Stella's husband Jacques and son Iko, and other relatives. Tilde was arrested by the Gestapo at one point for resisting when they looted the family apartment, but was released. They were able to get to Split a couple of months after Moshe, where they turned themselves in to the Italians. They were interned in a private home in a town in northern Italy, and had to report regularly to the police. In early 1943 Moshe got into an argument with the landlady, who evicted them. They were sent to Ferramonti in the south. This saved their lives: Ferramonti was liberated in September 1943 by the Allies while Jews in northern Italy became in severe jeopardy from the Germans and many there were arrested and deported to Auschwitz.

My father remembered the day the Salomons came to the camp, in May 1943. They caused quite a stir, as Moshe had managed to bring a lot of baggage, including stored food. My parents met in Ferramonti shortly after the Salomons arrived. I am guessing his romance with a daughter of a family with food helped him avoid starvation.

As my mother died when I was 14, I know less about her own experience in the camp. I know the Salomons lived in a family style barracks.

Life after Ferramonti

In July 1943 the Allies invaded Sicily and Mussolini's government fell. In early September they invaded the mainland. The Ferramonti prisoners woke up on September 9 to find the guards had fled. The camp was initially liberated by the British 8th Army, then occupied by American troops. Srecko and the Salomon family stayed for two months, during which Srecko formed a small band to play music and entertain the troops. Moshe worried, though, that the Germans, who had committed troops to Italy when Mussolini fell and were far more formidable opponents, could roll the Allied advance back down the peninsula, jeopardizing the Jews. Sicily seemed safer, as the Germans probably couldn't retake it amphibiously, and so the family left for Sicily in November 1943.

They crossed at the Straits of Messina and ended up in Palermo, where they squatted in an apartment vacated by an Italian general. They needed dishes and found a set of china there. We still have it and call it the fascist china. Moshe, who was handy and resourceful, tapped into a power line to provide electricity. There was tension between Moshe and my father over his involvement with my mother, and for a while my father lived in Palermo with Aunt Stella, her husband Jacques Medina and son Iko.

The Allies forced the Italians to let refugee Jews, who were not allowed to work, to attend university. My father and Uncle Nello began classes in Palermo while my mother went to work for British Naval intelligence. They found a Jewish foreigner more trustworthy than native Italians, whose loyalty under the circumstances, might be called into question. My father meanwhile started what would be a lifelong vocation, document translation, for extra money. He was contracted to translate the testimony of political prisoners who had been held by Mussolini from Italian into English although, he noted, he didn't really speak either language. He had help in the Italian from a professor neighbour who did it in return for getting a look at the testimony—who was saying what. As a gesture of thanks to the Allied troops for their liberation, Moshe organised a Passover *seder* for Jewish Allied troops in Palermo.

In 1946 the family moved to Rome, and my father enrolled at the University to study chemistry. The family lived not far from the Vatican. My parents married in 1947 and moved into their own place in a different neighbourhood. My father graduated with his PhD in 1948, third in his class. The family emigrated to the United States in 1949. My mother worked, as noted above, for the Joint in Rome. Her office was in the Barberini Palace and she climbed a Bernini staircase every day to get there. My father worked as a medical supplies salesman, calling on doctors. He also got hired to make Serbo-Croatian language broadcasts for the Allies into now-Communist Yugoslavia after Tito's regime took over in 1945.

My mother's brother-in-law Jacques and a few relatives, not allowed to work and not wanting to go to a Displaced Persons camp, supported themselves changing money, which was illegal at the time. Jacques stood outside the Italian foreign ministry at the Piazza Colonna and changed currencies for diplomats and military officers who needed it done. He would use hand signals across the square to his hunchbacked brother Andre, who sat in a cafe, who would make other hand signals to someone in the back, who actually had the money in various currencies in a bag. Jacques paid off police not to bother them.

Jacques had a friend who was a Jewish American soldier, who had arranged for the Medinas to be sponsored as immigrants by a young business couple in the soldier's hometown, Great Barrington, Mass. However, in 1947, the heat was on, and Jacques and his family needed to leave. They purchased citizenship in Brazil and moved to Rio. They meanwhile transferred the US visas and immigration sponsorships to my parents and the Salomons. The family left Italy in August, 1949, sailing to the United States on the SS Atlantic.

They stayed in Great Barrington a few weeks — their arrival in late August was noted in a local newspaper — and my dad found a job in a state medical lab at Harvard. He legally changed his name to S. Edmund Berger in the United States. Uncle Nello had won a scholarship to Massachusetts Institute of Technology and began school there, although he would later return to Turin, Italy to complete his studies there. My sister Ruth was born in 1951 in Boston. The family, including the grandparents, moved to Buffalo, NY later that year when my dad accepted a job at the National Aniline research lab there. It later became Allied Chemical and then Honeywell. Ed and Sulty became citizens in November 1954 and I was born a month later. My mother died of cancer in June 1969. My dad married Benis Gilden Chernoff in June 1970. They celebrated 50 years of marriage last year. My dad retired when he turned 65 in 1987, after 36 years at Allied Chemical. He went full-time with his moonlight career, technical translating, and continued to do that until he was 90. He died in December 2020 at the age of 98.

Dan Berger, Atlanta, Georgia, USA

Ed Berger, front row right, Ferramonti, 1942. His uncle Ernest Breder back row right

Ed Berger, top row far left, Ferramonti, 1942

Ed (centre front) 24.01.1943

Sultana and Ed's wedding 1947

Lisa (Lisl) and Henry Bernstein

It was a cold and bleak day on March 12, 1938 when Hitler marched into Austria, a day known as the Anschluss. Everything in my life changed from that day forward.

We lived in terrible fear of the Nazis, hearing the news on the radio and from friends and family of what was going on in the rest of Europe. We learned that Jews were being taken from their homes in Vienna and transported by trains to unimaginable and frightening places. We lived through Kristallnacht; we saw glass being shattered in shops and synagogues throughout Vienna. It was beyond horrifying.

We remained in our apartment in Vienna praying for the best but the fear of our family being taken away to a concentration camp became too much for my father to bear and in October 1939 he succumbed to a heart attack and died. So now at the age of 40, my mother became a young widow and my sister Anny and I were left without our father. The pain we all felt was excruciating which no words can adequately describe.

As we had anticipated, the Nazis came to our door and my mother, sister and I were forced to leave our apartment in Vienna with nothing but the clothes on our backs. They placed us in another apartment in the same vicinity together with another family whom we did not know.

By 1940, my mother had had enough and decided that we must escape from this horror. We needed papers from the Gestapo to leave the country which we somehow acquired and planned our journey. We travelled by train to Graz, a city southeast of Vienna situated on both sides of the Mur River, where we were met by someone who took us to stay in a stable with yet another group of people already in place. We slept on hay and remained there overnight, leaving the next morning with the group to cross the border to Zagreb which was in Yugoslavia at that time. We had to walk in freezing weather in very deep snow wearing only what we had on our backs which was not much and in worn out shoes without any snow boots to protect our feet. This trek was supposed to take approximately two days on foot.

After walking for six hours, we came across a soldier with a rifle standing at the top of the mountain who shouted at us in German, "Halt, or I will shoot." My poor mother wanted us to just leave her there in the snow and continue without her because she said she did not have the strength to go on, but my sister and I would hear nothing of the sort. We grabbed her by the arms and helped her to walk and like this we continued with her in tow. We turned around and walked back this time using a different route leading to Graz and went to yet another stable. The next day we tried to cross the border, but once again were stopped by a soldier who ordered us to return or he would shoot us dead. We later made a third attempt at crossing the border and this time we succeeded.

When we arrived in Zagreb, there were many cars waiting for our group and we had to jump into them quickly so that we could speed away as fast as possible. In Zagreb, we were placed in a house owned by a Jewish family. My sister was sent somewhere else in the area and I remained in this house together with my mother. Once again we left this place and went to live with another family where there was a husband, a wife, and three children and where we stayed for several months.

Hitler came once more and took away the husband who was never seen again.

We just had to escape. This time we would flee to Ljubljana, then a province of Italy which in 1941 was annexed by Fascist Italy and after 1943 occupied by Nazi Germany. We got hold of an Italian newspaper which we pretended to read in order to give the impression we were Italians so no one would bother us on the train.

We finally arrived in Italy and were instructed by Italian officials to stay in an Italian military station where we remained for two months. After that we were told to leave so they placed us in two rooms behind a garage with an outdoor toilet in Nizza Monferrato, a little commune in the province of Asti. We stayed there for two years during which I repaired stockings which I was paid for with food instead of money. We were so hungry and just wanted something to eat.

Once again, we were told we had to go to the police station where they informed us we would be placed in the concentration camp, Ferramonti di Tarsia, Calabria. We arrived there in May 1943. I met my husband in the camp and we married after knowing one another for only five months. When the war ended, we still remained in the camp because we had nowhere else to go. I gave birth to my daughter who was born in a nearby hospital in Cosenza. We returned to Ferramonti with our new baby girl who we called Ruth.

After liberation, my husband and brother-in-law left Ferramonti to find a business for themselves. They went to Rome where they met a man at the train station whose name was Salvatore and who beckoned them to go with him. Salvatore had a little house in Rome which he had occupied from some Fascists. We stayed there with Salvatore for 6 months until the Fascist family that owned this house returned.

Once again we found ourselves on the move but my ever resourceful husband found us a beautiful and large apartment in the centre of Rome on Via Villetri and we moved in. While in Rome, my beloved mother developed ovarian cancer at the age of 46 and I very sadly lost her too.

My husband started an import/export business and did very well, while my sister's husband opened a hotel in the centre of Rome and also became successful. The hotel is still in existence today and is run by my sister's son and her grandson. We remained in Rome until we moved to New York where I had a maternal aunt and uncle who lived in the Italian section of Brooklyn so we moved in with them. I was miserable and wanted to return to Italy. I did not know the English language and everything was so strange for me, but my husband asked me to give it a chance and thankfully, I did.

After about a year, we left Brooklyn and my husband once again found us a lovely apartment in Washington Heights in upper Manhattan in New York City. He went into the city every day and struggled to look for some sort of work but instead, he started a business of his own.

I got pregnant and we were very happy in Washington Heights where we met many friends we knew from the war.

Several years later when we were already settled, tragedy struck us like lightning when my younger daughter developed a malignant brain tumour. She passed away exactly two years after her diagnosis, just as the doctors predicted. It was the worst time of my life and my husband and I suffered greatly from losing our child who had been the picture of perfect health. My little daughter Loly was filled with such vitality and zest for life before the cancer took her away from us.

The loss of a child is something that parents never get over and assuredly, I never will. Time passes and somewhat helps lessen the pain, but this is a type of pain that remains with you for the rest of your life.

A couple of years after we lost our little girl, I gave birth to twin boys which we felt was nothing short of a miracle and my older daughter was so happy to have two little brothers.

The apartment became too small for all of us and one of our very good friends told us about a house for sale in Queens a block away from where he lived. We bought the house, moved in, and had a wonderful life there with a great many friends. The house was always filled with visitors. We enjoyed many happy occasions there.

After several years had passed my husband developed heart problems. One evening, I received a terrible call from his friends where he had gone to play cards. They told me he had collapsed on their porch after telling them he wasn't feeling well and wanted to go home. He never made it back to me. The ambulance came to take him to the hospital where he sadly passed away. The friends, I might add, continued with their card game as though nothing had happened after the ambulance had left. I could never face these people after that and wanted nothing to do with them ever again.

Life as I knew it would never be the same.

When a couple of months passed, I decided I had to go on for my children's sake as well as for my own. I picked myself up and went to work every day in my husband's business. My twin boys had already started working there with their father after they had graduated college so I wasn't alone. This went on for many years until my sons decided to sell the business and went their separate ways.

Today, my family has greatly expanded and all my children, grandchildren and great grandchildren come to visit or stay the weekend. I love having them here and they're always so happy to spend time with their grandma or nonna as some call me. It's a big treat for all! My daughter is a tremendous help and sees to all my needs so that I am able to manage happily on my own. People as well as my own family have always thought of me as a strong woman and perhaps there is some truth in that.

Lisa Bernstein, Flushing, Queens, USA

Lisl and Henry's wedding, Ferramonti, mother Lola, right

Family Bernstein

Henry Bernstein

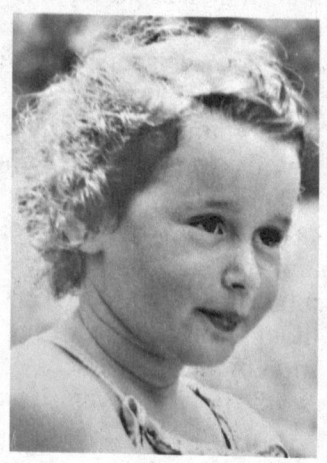
Loly

Lisa now

Ruth Bernstein-Bieber

I was born in Calabria in the southern part of Italy to my parents, Lisa (Lisl) and Henry Bernstein. My parents were still in the camp in Ferramonti but had to go to a hospital so my mother could give birth. Once I was born, we had to return to Ferramonti and remained there until liberation. When the war finally ended, my parents took the train from Ferramonti together with my mother's sister, Anny Lazar and her husband, Ernesto Lazar, to Rome where they resettled and started new lives. My uncle decided to go into the hotel business and ultimately bought a hotel called Hotel Delle Muse which is in Rome in the quiet and residential section of Parioli located on 18 Via Tommaso Salvini. This charming hotel is still in existence today managed and run by my uncle's son, Giorgio Lazar along with one of Giorgio's sons. My father went into the import/export business in Rome and did quite well. I was sent to a Catholic school and can still recall how strict the nuns and priests were with ruler in hand ready to strike out at any child they felt was misbehaving. I hated going to that school and threw up every morning from nerves. To this day, I still get very nervous and become jittery when having to go anywhere outside my comfort zone, almost as though I am still a child in my inner soul.

After several years, my parents decided to move to "North America" which was how America was referred to in Italy at that time. The Lazars remained in Rome feeling they had an allegiance to the Italian people because they were good to them during the war and so they continued with their hotel business. My parents had initially planned to move to Australia but plans got changed and we boarded a ship and sailed to New York. My mother had a maternal aunt and uncle who lived in the Italian section of Brooklyn and with whom we lived for less than a year. I was sent to a public school not speaking a word of English. The only languages I knew at that time were Italian and German since these were the languages my parents spoke at home. My mother is from Vienna and my father was from Poland. I don't recall when I first began to learn to speak English, but somehow I did. Strangely, the one thing I recall from that school is that awful smell of the little containers of milk they used to serve the children at lunch. For years thereafter I could not stomach milk but got over it later in life.

After several months went by my father found us a beautiful apartment in a lovely building in Washington Heights in uptown Manhattan and we happily left my mother's aunt and uncle's house and began our lives once again.

My father went into the city every day to look for a business he could get into which he eventually did. Leave it to the Holocaust survivors. They pulled themselves up by the bootstraps and many became very wealthy and quite successful. My mother got pregnant and gave birth to my beautiful sister, Loly, and I was so happy and excited to have a sibling. My parents then enrolled my in a yeshiva, conveniently located up the block from our apartment which I attended for 6 years.

When my sister was ready to start school, my father at that particular time could not afford to send us both to this yeshiva because the tuition had become too expensive, so he asked me how I felt about attending public school. I jumped at the opportunity because I did not like the yeshiva so I started public school where I was much more content and where I made many friends.

When my sister was 5 years old, she complained of having terrible headaches. My parents took her to the best doctors in New York and she was diagnosed with a malignant brain tumour. She underwent chemotherapy and lost her sight. My parents sent her to blind school until she became too sick to attend. She then lost her hearing and her ability to walk. I recall my poor mother refusing to put my sister in the hospital, insisting she would be able to give her better care and attention at home, which she most certainly did. My mother nursed my bedridden sister for about 2 years until the cancer took her life and she died in her little bed. I will never forget that very tragic day which continues to haunt me and will for the rest of my life. As I write this, tears fill my eyes as it is unbearable to think about what can happen to a young and innocent child who appeared to be the picture of good health. I can still remember the hearse driving down the street and my father's gut wrenching cries as I watched this procession unfold before my very eyes from my best friend's window in our building. My friend was 2 years older than I but did not have the words to comfort me, as if there were any. For some reason, my parents did not take me to the cemetery and to this day, I don't know why. Perhaps it was to shield me from the awfulness of it all. I could ask my mother, but the tragedy still lives within us, so much so, that I do not like bringing up this topic for fear of dredging up those terrible memories and making my mother feel the sadness all over again.

A couple of years after Loly's death, my mother got pregnant but unfortunately had a miscarriage. After a few months passed, my mother got pregnant again and gave birth to twin boys which my parents believed was a miracle considering all they had been through with my sister, Loly. Our apartment suddenly became too small for 5 people so my father bought a house in Queens but waited to move in until I graduated high school.

Queens was so pretty. I recall looking out the window and thinking that the block we now lived on looked like a picture postcard. I started college and my parents had a wonderful and happy life there with many friends who were also Holocaust survivors with similar backgrounds, but I was not happy. After my sister died and we moved to the house, my father decided to become very religious and I was not used to all the rules and restrictions that I was now faced with. It was a big change from the way of life I knew and was used to. Not to mention, being the child of Holocaust survivors was never easy to begin with.

My parents were very strict with me and I felt trapped. I was 19 when I met a man 20 years my senior who I later on discovered was the same age as my mother. Needless to say, my parents were very much against my being with him for reasons other than his age, and tried everything they could to prevent this, but I did not listen and left the house with a lot of drama.

I got married to him and my sweet baby boy, Scotty, was born, but the marriage did not survive. While in the midst of a divorce, my precious son died at the age of 3 due to medical issues that I cannot talk about to this very day. The pain of losing my little boy still lives within me and never goes away even after all these years. I know I will take this heartache to my grave.

I remarried many years later and was not even married one year when my second husband suffered a massive heart attack and died in our home. A month later, I lost my father too. It was all much too much trauma and just too much to bear!

Today, I live alone and am happily independent. I don't know if I will every remarry, but life sometimes has a way of surprising you. My mother lives by herself in the house she shared with my father and where my twin brothers grew up. My mother has always been a very strong woman and is the matriarch of our family. She manages her own household, still drives, cooks, cleans, and is in good health. She is an exceptional woman and everyone likes and admires her. Many of her good friends and neighbours have unfortunately passed away, but we are a large family now and the grandchildren are plentiful. I see my mother several times a week, speak with her daily and we are very close. My brothers are married and each has many children. The grandkids call their Grandma weekly and see her as often as possible or they video chat with her on her computer. There are tremendous differences in lifestyles between my brothers and I because of their religious upbringing but we try to accept one another as we are and somehow, life goes on!

Ruth Bernstein-Bieber, USA

Little Ruthie

Henry and baby Ruth

Young Ruth

Ruth today

Maurizio Chotiner

Maurizio Chotiner (my father) was born into a Jewish family near Lvov, Galicia, on March 25, 1908.

He died in 1961, at the age of 53, when I was only 8 years old, and as he never told me about his past, what I know is from other sources.

My mother, Marianna Klein, was born on April 14, 1919 in Oradea Mare, Transylvania. After having begun her medical studies in Transylvania she arrived in Italy in 1945 after the war without any documents. She was allowed to resume her medical studies at Pavia University if she passed exams in anatomy, physiology, biochemistry, microbiology, pathology and so on. She succeeded and even finished her specialization in the School of Dentistry.

My father studied medicine at the German university of Prague until 1933; then he continued in Italy, finishing medical school in Parma in 1934 with the top marks of 110 out of 110.

Both my parents had studied Greek and Latin in high schools, so they had no problems with the Italian language.

My father was a physician and a dentist, and two rooms in our apartment in Pavia were his dental surgery.

My mother too was a physician and dentist, and started working in his office when my father's health deteriorated. He suffered from heart problems, which worsened when he was in Ferramonti camp. He needed heart treatment in Perugia or Arezzo, but the fascist authorities refused to let him go.

I remember that a patient of his was a violinist in the orchestra of Pavia. One day instead of hearing the usual noise of the old dental low-speed drill, I heard the beautiful sound of a violin coming from the surgery. I went to investigate. When I entered the room to my amazement I saw my father playing the patient's violin. I did not even know he could play as we did not have a violin at home.

My father was the eldest of four brothers and one sister. The second brother was Adolf, the third was Rubin. Both of them were murdered in the Shoah, as were their parents, my grandparents.

I remember that my father had a collection of large books written in Hebrew, which he could read.

I like to remember walks with my father in the park of the Castello Visconteo, and along the Ticino River, when he used to teach me how to recognise different trees and birds.

My father realised that the situation in Europe was getting worse, so in 1936 he went back to Lvov to try to persuade his family to come to Italy. He worked in the Jewish Hospital and in his private practice in Lvov, until 1937, when he went back to Novi Ligure, Italy.

Only his brother Rubin came to Pisa where he also studied medicine, but at the end of 1938, the racial laws prevented him from continuing his studies, so he had to go back to Lvov.

My father worked in his dental practice in Novi Ligure until 1940.

On June 10, 1940, Italy declared war on France, and my father was arrested and sent to the concentration camp of Campagna in Salerno.

On August 18, 1940, he was sent from Campagna to Ferramonti, in Calabria.

On November 4, 1940, he was granted a permit (number 442/21624) to practise dentistry in Ferramonti concentration camp.

On November 19, 1940 he was transferred to the nearby village of San Marco Argentano, where an interesting tale unfolds. A rather beautiful woman by the name of Sonia Kuschlin was receiving unwanted attentions from a local tailor, Amerigo Borrelli, who had been captivated by her beauty when working in Ferramonti. The tailor managed to separate her from her husband (Jakob Merzer) who remained in Ferramonti.

My father gave the tailor a beating. The tailor escaped from my father and hid inside a large bread oven (which was off at the time), and refused to get out until the arrival of the Carabinieri and a safe escort away from my father. This is a local story still remembered by the inhabitants of San Marco Argentano!! This is all documented in the note number

448/304128 of the Direzione Generale della P.S., Divisione Affari Generali e Riservati, sezione terza, about the note number 03525-Gab dated April 11, 1941 that was sent from the R. Prefettura of Cosenza to the Ministry of Interior in Rome. In this document the tailor is called "un giovane dabbene del luogo", and the Prefetto of Cosenza (Mr De Sanctis) decided to take Mrs Sonia Kuschlin back to her husband in Ferramonti di Tarsia concentration camp as a matter of urgency.

Borrelli then wrote to Guido Buffarini Guidi, Minister for the Interior in Rome, asking for him to send my father back to Ferramonti also, so my father returned to Ferramonti, until he was transferred to Potenza and later to Avigliano where he remained until the end of the war.

Later he moved to Pavia where he married my mother. I was born 1952 in Brooklyn USA, where I grew up.

Giorgio Chotiner, Jerusalem

My grandmother Fanny Schrage, aunt Emilia, uncle Rubin, my father Maurizio (seated) uncle Bernardo, grandfather Schulim (seated), uncle Adolf.

ID for Medical School, Prague, 20 October 1928

My father Maurizio Chotiner

My mother Marianna Klein

Shlomo and Anna Danziger

Shlomo Danziger married Anna (née Kupferman) in Magdeburg Germany in 1920. He was born in Bedzin, Poland and involuntarily brought to Germany by the German army who conscripted him as a teenager for factory work in support of the First World War effort. At the end of the war, a secular Shlomo enjoyed life in Germany better than in Poland. Ironically, on Kristallnacht it was his wife who was arrested and deported.

Anna's father and brother both died from wounds suffered while fighting for the Germans in the war. But Anna's mother had had the bad luck of going into labour with Anna while visiting her sister in Poland in June of 1900. Anna and her mom returned to Germany after a week, but that circumstance made her stateless to the Nazis who deposited her in no man's land in November 1938.

Shlomo spent the next months sending his 15 year old daughter to England on the Kindertransport and his 13 year old son to Holland, with the false hope of reuniting with them after retrieving Anna and then emigrating to America. But the family would never all be together again, though all survived the war. Shlomo and Anna tried every exit door to leave Germany before finally having the incredible good fortune of the Jewish Agency buying them a spot on a river boat that would sink and leave them and all the passengers on a deserted island in the middle of the Aegean. But when they boarded the Pentcho in May of 1940, the ill-conceived hope was that the wretched, overcrowded steamboat would take them to Palestine.

But in fact, the Jews on the shipwrecked Pentcho were rescued by the Italian navy and ultimately brought to the Ferramonti Camp in February/March of 1942. The Jews left behind in Magdeburg would end up sent to Theresienstadt and the Warsaw Ghetto. Anna spent her time doing what any Jewish mother would. She tried to locate her children, as Jews in Ferramonti had the luxury of correspondence with the outside world. It would seem that she was unsuccessful at this as her daughter had turned 18 and "aged out" of the Jewish home for *Kindertransporters* she was in, and her son had gone into hiding in Holland with false papers. It is not difficult to imagine their distress at the uncertainty. In fact, by the end of 1942, escaped concentration camp survivors who wound up in Ferramonti told of the terrible fate that was befalling the Jews of Europe. The postcards arriving for Anna from Jewish agencies in Switzerland tried to lift her spirits, suggesting that "no news might be good news".

Ultimately Shlomo and Anna were liberated with the other Jews of Ferramonti in September of 1943 and went to Bari Italy. As I understand it, they helped the British interrogate/act as translators for German POWs. By June of 1944 they would finally arrive in Palestine, thanks to the British. Their son would join them there a few years later, before leaving for America in 1956. They would not see their daughter again until 1958, in England.

There are times when I share my paternal family's Holocaust story that the listener will comment on their "luck". 'Oh, they were lucky to be in Germany and could see what was coming and have a chance to escape that Polish Jews never had. Lucky to have boarded a boat that sank in the Aegean leading them to be interned in Ferramonti and not a "real" concentration camp. Lucky to be allowed into Palestine when it was near impossible to do so due to British restrictions and then to be in Israel at the founding.' I bite my lip because I appreciate the point being made. In the binary choice of living or dying, they lived, unlike six million other Jews. But so much of what we appreciate as life was stolen from them.

For starters, as German Jews, the Holocaust started for them in 1933. The country that my grandmother sacrificed a brother and father for in the First World War, now viewed her and her family as a malignancy. Friends suddenly evaporated and crossed the street rather than encounter them. Their children were beaten up and made to drink urine in school before being kicked out completely. They were robbed of the store they owned and their savings, and made the excruciating decision to send their children away. The worst loss was that—their family was stolen.

Those children grew up without the guidance of their parents and without an education. They were forced to emigrate to countries as unskilled immigrants and were consigned to lives of hard work and poverty. Their dreams for their children were stolen.

Shlomo and Anna were hardly Zionists; they had declined an opportunity to go to Palestine before the Nazis. Boarding the Pentcho was buying a lottery ticket that had an unknown prize which was much better than the death they saw as the certain end of staying in Germany or occupied territories. But along that journey and through to their liberation day, the fear of death never stopped gnawing at their souls. The longing for their children never stopped tugging at their hearts. Their choice to go to Palestine was little different from choosing to get on the Pentcho. It put more distance between the Germans and them. And unlike the option of going to Oneonta, NY, they would not have to live inside a fence again, waiting to be sent home to a place that would never be home again.

The arrival of their son Arthur in Palestine was a blessing. Being able to see him married and hold their grandson, was a moment of grace and celebration in a life with too few of those moments. But from the moment Shlomo and Arthur were in Palestine they had to pick up a gun. They had to fight for their lives as they, once more, found themselves surrounded by forces intent on exterminating them. Arthur's wife, a survivor of the camps, who lost every member of her large nuclear family, could no longer bear seeing Arthur put his uniform on and walk out the door, not knowing if she would see him again, or if her own son would be murdered. She begged him to leave and in 1956, Shlomo and Anna lost their family again. Arthur and family got a visa to the United States, but they did not.

They waited and waited for a visa to come through but when it did not, they made an incredibly difficult decision. Poor, and ageing, Germany was beginning to pay meagre reparations to Jews. They offered to pay double reparations to any German Jew who would return to Germany. In this way they hoped to re-establish some Jewish community in the cradle of Nazism. Shlomo and Anna returned to Hanover, Germany in 1958, seeing it as their only hope of avoiding abject poverty. On their trip to Germany, they stopped in England and saw their daughter Marie for the first time in 20 years, along with four grandchildren. Again, from 1945 on, the trip might have been logistically possible but travel was a luxury item. It was beyond their means. Anna would also never see her sister in South America or her brother in New York again in her lifetime. It was a blessing they survived, but in a real sense they were lost to one another.

All the Danzigers were in poor physical and mental health. PTSD, the effects of years of malnutrition and lack of access to medicines and doctors, the stress on their body from the physical labour they were forced to choose as their life's work. Anna would die of a heart attack at the age of 60. Shlomo would be blinded by a stroke and need a cane to walk. There were no golden years after the war for them. They too were stolen.

Michael Danziger, grandson, USA

Young Shlomo (right)

Shlomo and Anna Danziger

Shlomo, left, with Cardinal, Ferramonti

Shlomo's Ferramonti ID card

Anna, Shlomo, grandson Alex, Israel 1954

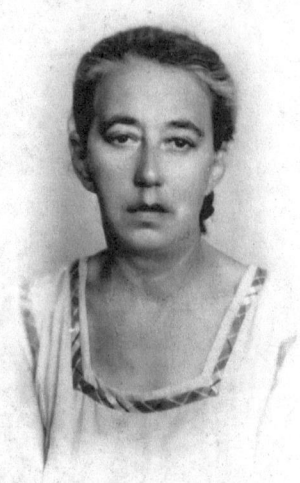

Anna late1950s

Riccardo Ehrman

I am an Italian journalist, to be precise, a *fiorentino*, a native of Florence, who as a child had been with his parents a "guest" of Ferramonti di Tarsia, the biggest fascist concentration camp (2-3000 internees) for enemies of the regime because we were certainly guilty of being Jewish. I have also acquired a certain professional renown after the war, having been credited for my contribution to the fall of the Berlin Wall.

In early 2021 the cultural publication, *Parchi Letterari*, published an issue dedicated to the former concentration camp in which it headlined a story referring to me as, "The child of Ferramonti who brought down the Berlin Wall." Of course I did no such thing. It is however possible that my questions on freedom of travel between the two Germanys at the famous East Berlin press conference of 9th November, 1989, were the spark that shocked, or reminded the GDR speaker Gunther Schabovski, who died of Alzheimer's years later, into taking out the "bomb" that he had in his pocket and read the announcement that changed the world.

My father, Jozef (Giussi) born in 1898 in Slobodka Lesna, near Cracow, and my mother, Jozefa (Jozka) born in Lwow, 1901, decided to expatriate to Italy to escape the anti-Semitic moves that were present in Poland long before the Nazi occupation. After my birth in Florence in 1929 everything went smoothly until 1938 when Mussolini issued his "racial laws" which dictated that all Jewish children were to be expelled from public schools. I was able to continue my studies in Catholic schools thanks to the personal involvement of the Archbishop of Florence, Cardinal Elia Dalla Costa. It must also be said — to their credit — that my teachers did not try to convert me to Catholicism.

After we arrived in Ferramonti, having travelled with armed police escort, the only pleasure was to find there the famous painter Michel Fingesten (born Finkelstein) a former companion of studies of my mother's at the University of Vienna which before the Anschluss was the only European university that accepted Jewish students. The Maestro gave my mother a souvenir of Ferramonti which was a terrific inked design of himself with a desperate expression with the background of barracks and barbed wire. He entitled it, "Calabrische Elegie". Just recently I thought that its rightful place would be in the museum created in Ferramonti and have donated it so that now it is the highlight of that worthy and very interesting institution.

It is very probable that the detention in the camp which was situated in Calabria, on the very south of Italy's peninsula, turned out to be a salvation for its inmates because the Nazi plans to transfer all by train to Germany, and to certain death, never came to fruition thanks to the lack of co-operation of the then Italian rulers. Much worse luck befell the thousands of Jews who had remained free in the big cities of Rome, Milan and Florence; they had been captured by the Nazis themselves and sent on a voyage with no return.

The last days before the liberation by Allied troops had been the worse because of the terrible hunger. Had it not been for the generosity of the Calabrian population who (some perhaps for profit) brought us help slipped under the barbed wire, while the guards looked elsewhere, our survival would have been much more difficult; on a very good day our food consisted of a small piece of dried bread dipped in water to make it palatable and one raw egg.

After the liberation we returned to Florence where I found work as a police reporter in a local newspaper, but the fact that in my youth—like in many Jewish families—I had been tutored in English and German made it possible for me in a few short years to jump from police reporter to foreign correspondent and in this role I have reported from the US, Canada, Germany, India and Spain. I retired to Madrid and still live there with my Spanish wife. Of course, I now also speak French and Spanish.

In the 11 years that I have been a Berlin correspondent for the Italian national news agency Ansa, I have never come across one single case of the local population trying to help the unfortunates in the many lagers. But then it is also true that while the fascist guards, mostly made up of local people who had enrolled in the militia to avoid army duty, looked the other way, the sadistic Nazi guards would have shot to kill.

Riccardo Ehrman, Madrid

Calabrische Elergie by Michel Fingesten

Riccardo Ehrman with his wife (behind) and Ferramonti representatives Simona Celiberti, Roberto Cannizzaro, Prof Teresina Ciliberti

Isacco Friedmann

Isacco (Iso) Friedmann was born on January 16, 1914 in Brody, in modern-day Ukraine. In the 1800s and early 1900s it was 70-90% populated by Jews with a minority of Ukrainians and Poles. It was an important commercial crossroads and was granted the privilege of a free port by the Austrian Emperor Franz Joseph.

Iso was a very bright child. With his paternal grandfather, a Hassid, he attended synagogue and read Hebrew from an early age. Iso's mother's family had a tavern and his father Leone was a tailor.

At the age of 27, Leone became a soldier in the Austrian army under Emperor Franz Joseph in the 1st World War (from 1914 – November 1918). Taken prisoner by the Italian army he was sent to Fort Begato in Genoa, where, knowing the language, he was employed as a translator.

By the end of the war, Leone had become enchanted with Italy and did not want to return to his homeland. He sent a message to his wife: "take the child and come!"

She checked with the rabbi who advised her to travel, seeing the increasingly negative situation towards Jews. (The Soviet-Polish war began in 1919 and also involved Ukraine until 1921).

This decision saved little Isaac and his mother, because all the Jews of Brody were deported and killed including 14 members of Iso's own family.

The journey to Italy took two years because in Prague Iso had caught typhus among other illnesses, which in those days was almost always fatal. In later years he would say jokingly: "I have not been sick again in my life because I have already made my contribution then."

They arrived in Genoa in 1921 and Iso, only 7 years old, immediately fell in love with the sea which remained his great passion. His mother remembered this time as the most beautiful of her life; they had only two rooms, but she had her husband and son and no anti-Semitism! Two more sons were born and they were financially secure.

His father Leone had started a business making waterproof coats for sailors. He would hire a boat to take him out to the ships to take their measurements, and since he was a man of his word, business went well and he was soon able to open his own men's clothing shop.

What the family valued most was the kindness of the Genoese towards the Jews. They said that on Fridays and Saturdays people greeted the Jews who went to the Synagogue, and they were also friendly with the priests.

Iso was happy to be able to go to school and did well in his studies, spoke the Genoese dialect and gave Italian lessons to his mother. After high school he began his medical studies specialising in neurosurgery. He was completely Italian and had many friends.

Meanwhile, he was captivated with the game of Bridge and at the hospital he and his colleagues played all through the night when they were on call, much to the surprise of the other staff who asked, "how do these junior doctors get on to the ward so fast, even at night?"

Everything changed with the introduction of the racial laws of King Vittorio Emanuele III on 5 September 1938. Jews lost their Italian citizenship and their children were not allowed to continue their schooling.

On December 15, 1938, Iso was also declared stateless, and was unable to continue his training with Prof Delisi, a famous neurosurgeon.

Iso, however, managed to graduate in Sassari on 11 July 1939 in medicine (Italian miracle!). He always remembered the words of the professor, who handed him the document. "I see from your name that you are going to face a difficult life, but you will see, this too will pass!" Courageous and consoling words. What hurt him deeply, however, was the attitude of some of his friends who crossed the street to avoid meeting him.

On 6 July 1940 he was escorted by the Italian police from his home in Genoa to the Principal Railway Station where he was sent in a locked wagon to Ferramonti di Tarsia camp where he remained for two years.

Late one night one of the camp administrators came to Iso for medical help. He had been suffering from hiccups for a long time and was desperate. Iso managed to cure the problem. As a 'thank you' he was given 'sick leave' and taken to *confino libero* in Lungro, where he had to report every day to the local police without any other obligations.

Locals soon came to the 'Jewish doctor' rather than their Italian doctor, paying in salami and pieces of silk. Of course, the local doctor denounced him and so the gates of Ferramonti were opened up once again until July 30, 1942.

The camp commander had a brother (who was, according to him, not very bright) who had to take his final exams. Iso offered to help him study. In History, for example, he told the boy to write, "Jews are people who do harm to our people and are inferior." The boy was shocked and exclaimed, "But doctor!" But Iso insisted, "just write it!"

He passed the exam because the theme on the Jews came up and Iso, again as a reward, was sent to Santo Stefano d'Aveto, in Liguria, again in *confino libero*, together with his dog Gilding, a gift from the commander. Just for fun, Iso had named the dog after the tenor Paul Gilding Gorin, who was one of his fellow internees in Ferramonti.

On November 11, 1943, he woke up in the night with a bad feeling. He could see in the valley below that soldiers from Rapallo were rounding up all the Jews they could find. They were to be sent to German concentration camps.

He remained in hiding in the mountains in Val Trebbia, until the spring of 1944, feeling hunted and without knowing where to eat and stop for the night. He remembered those winter months as a terrible nightmare until the end of his life.

He managed to get fake documents from the partisans, but he hardly ever moved from his hiding place which he had found in Genoa, afraid of being recognized.

On April 25 the Allies finally entered Genoa and the nightmare was over. When the remaining Germans were rounded up, he saw that they were all boys scared to death. He told them, "always remember, it was a Jewish doctor who treated you!"

After the war he became a very talented general practitioner and much loved by his patients. He was married happily to his German wife, Ingeborg, and they had a much longed-for son.

He was an athletic hiker who loved the mountains which he knew like the back of his hand.

Iso died surrounded by his family, loved and respected by everyone on January 13, 2017, three days before his 103rd birthday.

Ingeborg Friedmann, Genoa, 2021

Iso and Inge

Iso at 102

Iso with parents Gigi and little brother Josef about 1930

Iso in mountains

Iso in Ferramonti with his friends Dr Klein and Dr Ropschitz

Albert Goldfield

Ferramonti from the Perspective of a Child of an Internee

My father, Albert Goldfield, was born in 1913, near Czernowitz, now Ukraine, but spent almost all his childhood in Vienna. His father Israel Goldfield owned and operated a small clothing factory. My father attended the Hebrew Jewish high school in Vienna. He was in medical school when he was thrown out of a second storey window by Nazis shortly after the Anschluss between Austria and Germany in 1938. This made him realise he'd better leave Austria if he wished to stay alive and always said that their act of brutality was a good thing.

He never saw his parents again.

He eventually made his way to Italy.

After liberation he worked as a ship's doctor on boats to Palestine, finished his medical training at the University of Florence and married my mother, Liliana Mariani, (22.10.20), in 1949. They came to the U.S. when it became clear he would not find work in Italy without Italian citizenship. He was 46 before he had his first full time job!

We lived in Buffalo, New York, where my father worked as a pathologist till his retirement almost 20 years later. I moved my parents from Buffalo to Northampton MA after my mom had a stroke in 2000. My father died in 2007, aged 93.

Until I left home for college, my parents talked incessantly about the Holocaust and The War. At the same time, they also made every effort to enjoy their new life in America. Yet life was hard for them in the United States. They never acculturated and my father earned $100 a month for the first few years in the United States. My mother was an Italian Jew; my father an Austrian Jew. Their friends were almost all Italian (not Jewish). My mother always spoke about how she left her heart in Florence, her birthplace. They (and we) spoke Italian at home.

My father was extremely and understandably bitter towards the Austrians and anything German. He didn't like to speak German at all. In contrast, he only had positive things to say about Italians, their behaviour during World War II, and the Italian internment camps that he was in from 1940 to 1943. I am not claiming that all Italians were good to the Jews during the war (we know that wasn't true); this was just my father's experience. He always emphasized that the Italians living immediately outside the internment camps suffered as much as the internees—no one had food.

My Dad was in several Italian internment camps—most notably Notaresco, located east of Rome in Abruzzo, and Ferramonti di Tarsia, south of Naples in Calabria. He very much appreciated his time in Notaresco (I have letters that the director sent to my father after the war up until 1960) but had to leave when his finances (this part is not totally clear to me) did not allow him to stay. He was transferred to Ferramonti—a move that saved his life. Ferramonti was much less desirable than other internment camps because it was located on marshland and was malaria infested.

When Mussolini, Hitler's ally, abdicated in 1943, the Nazis took over all of Italy from Rome on north, including Notaresco. Any remaining Jews were sent to Nazi concentration camps and likely gassed on arrival. By the time Mussolini fell, the British had already liberated my father from his camp in Ferramonti which was south of Rome. So... my father was saved by not having any money!

My father always emphasized that Italian internment camps were not German concentration camps. He kept in touch with several fellow Ferramonti internees living throughout the world and remarkably found a husband and wife internee couple living in the same town, Buffalo NY, who eventually settled in the U.S. Both families met when I was about 10. We hung out periodically until I went to college. Amazingly I reconnected with the daughter, Ruth Goldston (née Berger) 50 years later at a Jewish week-long learning institute.

Regarding my own feelings about my parent's wartime experiences, I was in Israel in the 1980s at the same time, accidentally, at a conference of Holocaust survivors and their children. I remember asking myself did I qualify as a child of

Holocaust survivors. Did my parents "suffer enough" to be considered as Holocaust survivors. I went and, though I had started down this path well before, I began a personal journey of reading thousands of books about the Holocaust, as part of an effort to try to better "understand" what my parents went through. When my own children were growing up, rather than listening to a Holocaust survivor (they had my parents for that) I tried to take a different tack and brought people who rescued Jews to Northampton MA, the town I lived in with my wife and children. These remarkable human beings, also known as righteous Gentiles (the term used by Yad Vashem, the Israel Holocaust "authority"), made incredibly heroic decisions, including killing Nazis or prostituting themselves to Nazis to protect Jews. They stayed with us and lectured at the local schools and synagogue. My children saw courage face to face in our home.

As part of this same personal "search", in 1996 I went to Ferramonti with my wife and children. Much of the camp was destroyed years before to make way for a freeway. During that trip, we also met in the nearby city of Cosenza, Carlo Spartaco Capogreco, a paediatrician by profession but also an excellent historian who wrote one of the principal books about the history of Ferramonti camp. At lunch, I pointed out to him one of the pictures in his book, a photo of the Ferramonti parliament (yes there was a parliament in Ferramonti); my father was in the parliament and was in that picture. The notion that there was a parliament in an internment camp — well that was Italy — then and now. This explains why my father always felt very nostalgic about his time in Ferramonti. He did not have it easy at all; people were hungry; but till his dying day he said this was nothing compared to what happened to his mother Dora Goldfield, widowed after her husband's death from a heart attack, who was deported by the Nazis from her home in Vienna. Throughout his life, he constantly quoted from the last sentence of her last postcard, that I now have, that she sent before she was gassed in Treblinka: "my only wish is to have a little piece of bread."

Norbert Goldfield, MD., Springfield, MA.

Albert (L) in Notaresco

Albert in Ferramonti Parliament, centre back with beard

Albert Goldfield

Albert seated with cap. Parents on back row

Albert with grandson 1984

Albert with mother Dora

Richard and Else Goldstein

This is in memory of my grandparents. I knew my grandmother but not my grandfather. It is my pleasure to tell the story of my German grandparents who ended up in 1942 in Ferramonti camp. My grandfather, Richard Goldstein, was born in Cottbus, Germany, to Paul and Hulda Goldstein. He was born on March 30, 1874, and had two brothers, Arthur and Erich. Several generations of the Goldstein family lived in Cottbus.

My grandfather was a merchant who bought and delivered goods such as bananas and wine throughout the city. He had carriages and horses. He stayed in Cottbus until 1940. He suffered several anti-Semitic incidents. In the course of one, he was flung from a moving streetcar.

My grandfather married my grandmother, Else Goldstein, née Leipziger, born on January 26, 1887. They married in Cottbus on July 11, 1911. They had one child, my mother Rita. She left Germany in 1935 for Palestine. My grandparents visited her in 1937 but they did not like living in Palestine and returned to Germany to remain in Cottbus. It is said that my grandmother had a beautiful voice and sang in a choir.

In 1940, after World War II broke out, they were forced to leave and managed to reach Bratislava on the Danube. They boarded the ship Pentcho with the goal of reaching Palestine. The Pentcho experienced many hardships along the way. Eventually, after almost 2 years, the passengers ended up in Ferramonti camp in southern Italy.

Unfortunately I do not know anything about the lives of my grandparents in the camp. My grandfather died in Ferramonti on January 10, 1943. I obtained his death certificate, written in Italian, from an employee of the Holocaust Museum in Washington, DC who worked on a research project on Ferramonti. The camp was liberated by the Allies in September, 1943. My grandmother managed to leave Italy in 1944 and reach Palestine via Egypt. She arrived on the day I was born, June 5, 1944.

Again, my grandmother did not like living in Israel. Her sister, Friedel Heckscher who lived in Milwaukee, USA, invited her to come to live nearby. She accepted the invitation. In Milwaukee she worked as a housekeeper, living with a nice family. Later she accompanied this family to New York where she lived with them for 26 years, until 1970. She visited my parents in Jerusalem for my Bat Mitzvah in 1956 and another time we met up with her on a trip to Paris and Switzerland.

My grandmother did not tell us anything about those four hard years between 1940 and 1944. Many Holocaust survivors did not want to talk about what happened to them during that time. My grandmother had a nephew named Helmut Heckscher who heard a few things about that period and brought to my attention the book "Odyssey" by John Bierman. (Helmut Heckscher wrote a book entitled "Uprooted: The Memoir of Helmut Heckscher from Hamburg to the Kindertransport to America.") I read Bierman's book at the Holocaust Museum. He described how the ship Pentcho left Bratislava in May 1940 and was lost, due to a boiler explosion, in Italian controlled territory. The refugees on board were held in a camp on Rhodes until January 1942 before being transferred to the Ferramonti camp in February of that year.

In 1970 my parents invited my grandmother to come to Israel and she agreed. She lived in Kfar Shmaryahu at a senior home called Neve Aviv. She became sick and we had to move her to be near us in Jerusalem. She died in Jerusalem on July 28, 1973.

I visited Cottbus eight times and found a man who remembered my grandfather and a classmate of my mother. The two of them became my good friends.

I have recently learned more about life in Ferramonti and have welcomed the opportunity to share what I knew about my grandparents. Although I do not know much about their life stories, I would like to see their memory honoured and preserved for future generations as a part of the history of German Jews.

Granddaughter, Alisa Barkett, Silver Spring, Maryland, USA

Rita Goldstein and mother Else c1920

Else Goldstein

The Goldstein business in Cottbus

Alisa Goldstein 1964 IDF

Else Goldstein at Alisa's wedding 1971

Stefan Greiwer

Excerpt from, "Ferramonti: Salvation behind the barbed wire", by D. H. Ropschitz

"Stefan (Salomon/Shlomek) Greiwer was a polished and handsome young man. Though his looks were somewhat delicate, he could be very firm and authoritative when the need arose. He was an aesthete, much interested in the Muses as well as the art of good living. A pallid complexion contrasted sharply with raven black hair which he wore to one side, revealing a forehead of marmoreal pallor. Dark brown, penetrating eyes had a sharp vivid expression, in harmony with a sensitive aquiline nose. He was always impeccably dressed. A superficial observer might have taken him for a dandy, but there was a lot more to him than his sophisticated exterior suggested.

He was born on 5th June 1913 in Bochnia, a provincial town in Poland. His father Wolf, a wealthy textile industrialist, and mother Lea Sheindl Banach (born Poland 1888), had great expectations of their son. Like most Jewish parents who have acquired a measure of wealth, they wished him to enter one of the professions, preferably the one most honoured by Jewish hearts: medicine.

Stefan was a sickly child who at the age of fourteen had contracted rheumatic fever, which was said to have left him with some damage to his mitral valves. His parents were inclined to wrap their only child in cotton wool, but Stefan's independent spirit protested against their smothering. Although he had to abandon the more strenuous forms of sport on doctor's orders, he nonetheless took up soccer's less taxing position as a goalkeeper.

After matriculation his parents decided to send him abroad. Their choice fell on Montpellier, which had a renowned medical faculty. It was hard to send their only child away from home, but Numerus Clausus, that unofficial limit on the number of Jewish students, as well as the sickening anti-Semitism in Polish universities, helped them in their resolve.

Papa Greiwer was an intelligent man. He feared an excessive attachment between mother and son, and his own life experience had taught him the importance of stamina and moral toughness. It was imperative for the young 'loshak', the colt – as he called him affectionately – to escape his mother's overprotectiveness. Besides, there was also the question of prestige. It would be nice to say casually to his friends, "My son? Oh yes! He's studying medicine in the South of France. At Montpellier, the town of Nostradamus."

Young Stefan enjoyed his student days in France immensely. There he'd acquired an extra polish of charm and urbanity. His French became fluent, losing its textbook flavour. To Mama Greiwer it was an endless source of pride to listen to her son's French chatter during the summer holidays when she paraded him in the 'mondaine' circles of their small native town.

In those pre-war days provincial towns with a minimum of 'high life', a modicum of vice and some cultural interests regarded themselves as a 'Little Paris,' which made them feel superior, sophisticated and worldly. French was the second tongue of the Polish nobility and intelligentsia and proficiency in it was the hallmark of refinement.

To complete his education, both medical and general, Stefan decided to complete the second half of his medical training in Italy, dividing the four remaining years between Modena and Genoa. He qualified in 1939, barely nine months before Italy's declaration of war when his native Poland had already been invaded by German and Russian forces.

There was nowhere else to go, so he'd stayed in Italy hoping for the best...."

During his medical studies in Genoa, Stefan had developed a close relationship with a woman who appears in many photos, one of which is included here. Her name and what became of her is unknown. They are pictured together in Nice. He was certainly a handsome young man, in his late 20s, enjoying life on the Riviera and as a young medical student would have been quite a catch. Then the racial laws came and that put an end to his medical career.

So Stefan arrived in Ferramonti in July 1940 along with the first transport from Genoa with Henry Ropschitz and Isacco Friedmann among others; soon the three doctors, referred to as The Triumvirate, established a close rapport.

From further descriptions of him in the book quoted above, it seems Stefan was a charming, likeable and thoughtful young man, a peacemaker, who spent much of his time reading and keeping a low profile. While Henry and later Isacco both became heads (capi) of their respective camerata, Stefan was less interested in making a name for himself. He enjoyed playing cards and chess with his friends and was respected by his companions for his intelligent and perceptive disposition. But he did like football and a certain married lady who had befriended him. These were to be his downfall.

An important football match was to be played in Ferramonti in June 1941 despite the internees being half-starved. Because of his rheumatic fever, Stefan always played in goal so he'd acquired considerable expertise in that position and now he offered himself as goalie in the match: Poland vs The Rest of The World. A sudden change of game-plan meant Stefan was called upon to play on the wing. He over-exerted himself in a desperate bid to defend his goal and impress his lady, but also sustained a sharp kick in the chest which led to a pulmonary embolism after the match. On 19th June 1941, aged 28, less than one year after his arrival, Stefan Greiwer died on the dusty earth of Ferramonti. The shock and grief at his loss was indescribable. By now, he had become a much loved and admired character. The manner of his passing was so sudden—a young doctor with so much promise—that he should die in such a manner was heart-breaking. The Triumvirate was no more.

After his death he was buried in the local cemetery in Tarsia but over the intervening years space for Catholic graves was paramount; Jewish graves and headstones were removed. There is nothing to commemorate Stefan Greiwer's life or his death. His parents were killed in the Holocaust most probably after his death in Ferramonti. There remain some blood relatives in Israel, notably Nira Banach Ben Naim in Haifa, who has been able to supply some of the wonderful photos of the young Stefan—or Shlomek—as he was known in her family.

But for most of the world, Stefan Greiwer was just another casualty of war, lost without trace. My father being his close friend was presumably given his worldly goods, which is why I have a small collection of his photos, seen below. I imagine they were in his wallet or even by his bed at the time of his death. I feel privileged to have these, his precious possessions, from his last day on earth and to shine a small light on his existence through this publication.

My father, his friend, died 35 years ago, before his own book on Ferramonti was published. I feel honoured to share these photos and stories so we don't forget the name and the person who was Dr Stefan Greiwer.

Yolanda Ropschitz-Bentham, Somerset, England

Stefan with mother Lea Scheindl Banach

Young Stefan/Shlomo

Dr Stefan Greiwer

At Beau Rivage, Nice

Stefan Greiwer and lady friend

Dr Greiwer in Ferramonti kitchen

Yehoshua and Shoshana Halevy

Yehoshua Halevy (Alexander Citron)

Yehoshua Halevy was born Alexander Citron on September 26 1917, Yom Kippur, in the Hebrew year 5678, to parents Avraham and Rosa, in the small town of Berehovo (Берегове, Beregszász) in Slovakia (modern day Ukraine).

Yehoshua had four brothers and three sisters, all of whom emigrated to the USA between 1920 and 1930. The oldest sister who escaped the Nazis with her little daughter, and her husband who survived Auschwitz, joined the family in the 1940s. His nickname in the family was Bubi, but all his friends and acquaintances called him "Citi" (pronounced Tziti).

Yehoshua was interested in Zionism and in emigrating to Israel even as a young boy. He shared the ideals and beliefs of the Betar youth movement and in 1930, when not yet 13 years old, he organised a Betar summer camp for children of ages 13 to 16 in Berehovo. In the camp the children learned Hebrew, History and Geography of the Land of Israel. They were only allowed to use their Hebrew names, and if someone did not have a Hebrew name, he gave them one. When Zeev Jabotinsky, the founder and leader of the Revisionist Zionist movement, heard about the initiatives of this young lad, he was interested to find out more about him. In the years to come, the two met more than once in Betar and Revisionist-Zionist events.

After finishing school in the mid-1930s, he moved to Bratislava to study medicine at the university. He headed the Betar branch in Bratislava and organized illegal immigration ships to Israel ('illegal' because the British mandate in Palestine forbade any Jewish immigration there). In 1938, when Germany annexed Czechia and turned Slovakia into a protectorate, Jewish students were expelled from universities and Yehoshua, barely 20 years old, became head of the Betar movement in Slovakia, then the largest Zionist organization in Europe. He dedicated all his time to immigration efforts and commanded the last ship to sail out of Europe whose passengers made it to Palestine. There is no doubt that the leadership and youthful charisma Yehoshua displayed helped him lead the Pentcho and its immigrant-passengers to safety in the Land of Israel in May 1944.

Setting sail on the Danube from Slovakia presented many challenges and it took a year and a half before the passengers departed. When they lost all hope of buying a ship, Jabotinsky, at Yehoshua's personal request, nominated a special delegate to procure one, after the French refused to deliver the ship that the passengers had already paid for. The delegate did find an old tug ship in Italy and had it brought to Bratislava.

When the Slovakian rulers continually refused permission to set sail, Yehoshua, in his frustration, ordered the ship to depart without their permission.

The trip to the Black Sea along the Danube lasted five months, mainly because the Romanians turned them back half a dozen times. When they reached the Aegean sea, the Pentcho's steam boiler cracked and failed and the ship drifted until it hit the small rocky island of Chamilo Nisi from where they were saved by the Italians who shipped them to Rhodes. Thirteen months later the Italians moved them from Rhodes to Ferramonti di Tarsia, Calabria, thus protecting them from the Germans who demanded their extradition. They remained interned in Campo di Concentramento Ferramonti for more than two years.

The liberal and supportive attitude they experienced at the hands of the Italians was comforting. Yehoshua regularly organized cultural, educational, musical and sporting activities in Ferramonti. He was elected to lead and represent the Pentcho group there, and soon the camp climate was changed for the better.

In August 1943, in Ferramonti, Yehoshua married Shoshana who had been working with him in Bratislava, organizing and operating the Pentcho immigration. Shortly after their wedding, southern Italy was liberated by the British and American forces. As liberators, the British were finally prepared to allow the Pentcho passengers to enter and live in Palestine, and they did.

Yehoshua and Shoshana arrived with the first group that departed Italy and reached the Land of Israel in May, 1944. They settled in Nathanya, where they first lived in a wash-shed in a yard, and two years later they moved into an apartment of their own, with their baby boy.

Yehoshua joined the Etzel underground movement in Palestine. His family applied for him to go to Harvard Medical School. He was offered a place, but turned it down; having finally achieved his life's goal, he did not want to leave the Land of Israel. He found work in a diamond polishing factory, not far from home. Twice the British forces came to his home intending to arrest him, but on both occasions the informers' information was wrong. In order not to take chances of a third attempt to arrest him, Yehoshua left his home and moved to Germany in the summer of 1947, where he gathered holocaust survivors and organized their immigration to Israel. He continued doing this until the State of Israel was founded, in May 1948, when he travelled back home right away and joined the new Israel Defence Forces.

Soon after the war was over he dropped the family name Citron, given to them by the Spanish authorities a few centuries ago, and left the ancient, traditional family name Halevy in place.

After the 1948-49 war he managed the Betar and the Herut (Freedom) party in Nathanya, where he promoted and managed revisionist movement amenities such as medical services and a bank branch in Nathanya, as well as supporting the Betar youth movement there and the Betar Nathanya football team, then a top league team, where he also played as a front left winger.

Yehoshua was very active in the central leading group of the Herut party and was writing articles, serious and humorous too, in "Herut" daily newspaper. He also wrote a children's adventure book called "The Underground Children," printed every week in the "Herut for Youth" weekly magazine.

In the second half of the 1950s, a friend, who was managing a bank branch in Nathanya, offered Yehoshua a job there. He accepted, and for the first time in his life he earned enough to support his family (a wife, a son and a daughter). At the same time, Menachem Begin, leader of the Herut party who was the chief commander of the Etzel underground movement, asked him to be listed on a high level in the party's list of candidates for the forthcoming parliamentary elections. Yehoshua consulted his wife Shoshana. She told him that now, when he finally received a reasonable, stable salary, any gambling on politics was not good for him; as an honest man of high integrity he might not survive among all the tricks and manipulations of his colleagues in parliament. He listened to his wife and rejected the offer. Begin was not offended; he continued to be a close friend of Yehoshua, consulting with him often on many issues and was assisted by him. Begin was a guest at Yehoshua's son's Bar Mitzvah.

Apart from his various journalistic activities, Yehoshua wrote three books: "Habaita" ("Homeward"), the story of the Pentcho trip, including Ferramonti; "History of ČSR Betar" (ČSR = The Czechoslovak Socialist Republic), describing the stories of the Jewish National Zionist organizations in Czechoslovakia; "The Jewry of Berehovo-Beregszász in photos," describing the Jewish population in his home town, recorded on camera. Yehoshua kept working at the bank, was promoted several times, established new branches and eventually, managed one branch until he retired and worked in the bank's general headquarters in Tel Aviv.

Yehoshua Halevy died on Monday, January 26, 2009, in Nathanya.

His wife Shoshana died in December 1981, aged 66. They had two children, six grandchildren and eleven great-grandchildren.

Avner Halevy, Israel

Yehoshua Halevy
Age 20

Age 90

Shoshana Halevy (Rosalia Spiegel)

Shoshana Halevy was born Sara Rosalia Spiegel on October 9th, 1915, in Bratislava, Slovakia to a religious family. Her father was a wine merchant. She was the first-born child and had five younger brothers. The oldest brother, Isaac, joined the Republican fighters in the Spanish civil war, and later the Czech division of the Red Army. He was killed in Kiev, fighting against the Germans in WW2, holding off the advancing German tanks until his Czech battalion soldiers managed to retreat.

The second brother, Moshe, immigrated to Palestine in the 1930s, worked in agriculture, joined the Hebrew Division of the British army and fought with them against the Germans in WW2.

Rosalia's parents did not let her pursue further education, despite her obvious intelligence and aptitude for chemistry. Instead she played the piano and looked after her brothers. In her late teens she volunteered at the Betar office in Bratislava. The head of Betar, Yehoshua Citron, spotted Rosalia from across the road one day and said to his friend, "that's my future wife". Citron had no idea who she was but a few minutes later they met in the Betar Head office, and she began her work organizing emigration to Palestine.

In 1940, Rosalia asked her parents to join her in the last sailing from Bratislava, on the ship Pentcho, with her three young brothers. They refused, not surprisingly for European Jews at the time, but Rosalia persuaded them to let her take her two brothers with her, Eliezer (Onki) and Leopold (Yehuda). Her second-youngest brother, Joseph, remained to take care of his parents who refused to abandon their home, hoping that things would improve, but they did not. Joseph was sent to Theresienstadt concentration camp where he was murdered, and her parents were sent to their deaths in Auschwitz.

Yehoshua gave Rosalia a Hebrew name, as he did to all young Betar members. Her new name was Shoshana, meaning Rose.

The Pentcho* passengers began arriving in Ferramonti in February 1942. On August 17 1943, Shoshana and Yehoshua were married in Ferramonti.

Ten days later, an allied plane, mistaking Ferramonti for an enemy base, opened fire and machine gunned the camp, causing the deaths of four internees and injuries to many others. Soon after, the British and American forces liberated the entire area.

In May 1944 Shoshana and Yehoshua, along with Shoshana's two brothers Onki and Leopold, reached Palestine and settled in Nathanya. Onki, 22 years old and already married, found a job in a local factory, and Yehuda, 15, moved to Kibbutz Maaleh Hachamisha as a member of the youth group there.

Shoshana worked firstly in a bank in Nathanya and later in Rishon Lezion, in a branch opened by her husband. They had two children, six grandchildren and eleven great-grandchildren.

In December 1981, at the age of 66, while preparing to visit her one month old grandson in Haifa, Shoshana suffered a massive and fatal stroke.

Avner Halevy, Israel

Yehoshua and Shoshana Halevy

---

* The journey of the Pentcho is documented in the book "Homeward" by Yehoshua Halevy.

Kienwald Family

My grandfather Oskar Yehoshua Kienwald was born in Przemysl (Galicia) in 1888, the son of Leo Kienwald and Frjma Sonneck. He had a brother (name unknown) and their mother died young. Leo was a poor blacksmith who married a local woman with a child of her own, Mayer. The relationship between the boys and their father/stepfather was difficult and, probably in 1904/5, the three boys left home. Oskar went to live with his uncle Israel Kienwald in Jaroslaw where he trained as a tailor. He left Poland in 1908 and continued to train and then to practice as a ladies' fashion tailor in Innsbruck and then Zurich. In 1919 he returned to Jaroslaw where he was introduced to a distant cousin, Rachel Nadel (b. 1891), and they were married. The new couple moved to Bolzano (Bozen) in South Tyrol where they took up residence in 1920. Oskar became a renowned tailor and opened an atelier in that town. It is a matter of record that the Queen of Egypt, Nazli Sabri (wife of King Fu'ad I) ordered 13 dresses from him during one of her holidays in the Dolomites. My father Leonardo (Leo, Arieh) was born in 1921 and his brother Silvano (Ezra) in 1925.

In the summer of 1939, the family were expelled from Bolzano and took up refuge in Verona. They were arrested on 18 August 1940 and sent to Ferramonti where they remained until October 1941. They are officially listed as inmates of Ferramonti di Tarsia arriving 29th September remaining until 4th October 1941. What remain today are rather tenuous memories of accounts my father gave us in passing when we were children. I distinctly remember him telling us that my grandmother used to make *frittelle* which were sold by the boys outside their *camerata* and my grandfather used his tailoring skills to carry out repairs, etc. I also remember seeing a photograph of my father and his brother, who were trained to play the violin and the mandolin respectively, with two other young men, all holding an instrument and my sister and I believe that they may have been in some kind of musical ensemble at the camp.

In November 1941 the Kienwalds were evacuated to a small Tuscan village, Castelnuovo di Garfagnana. Their story during the final year of the war in Italy is told in a memoire written by my father, which I have translated and attached below.

After the war, my father met my mother, Celeste Di Segni, daughter of Amadio Di Segni and Eva Di Porto, in a hachshara in Bari. They were married in the Rome great synagogue. I was born in 1947 and my sister Tamar in 1949. Our family moved to Milan in 1950 and both my sister and I attended the Jewish school there up to matriculation. I attended university reading architecture at the Milan Polytechnic and my sister read biology in Jerusalem and Padua. I moved to London in 1972 and practiced as an architect until my first retirement in 2007, to take up the position of Chief Executive of the Federation of Synagogues until my second retirement in 2013. I subsequently attended a postgraduate course in archaeology at University College London where I obtained a diploma with distinction. My sister with her family (she married Renzo Cesana, a Venetian) emigrated to Jerusalem, where she currently lives. She has three children (all married) and 8 grandchildren. I have 4 children (three married) and 8 grandchildren.

Escape from Castelnuovo

It was 5th December 1943. The sky was grey, a harbinger of the incumbent tragedy....since everyone other than us ended up in Auschwitz. And they are no more.

Together, my father, mother, brother and I, Leonardo, were walking on a dirt road in the Turrite valley, Italy, distancing ourselves from the dreaded police station. The previous day an order issued by the *carabinieri*, commanded every Jewish person in town to assemble at their headquarters by eight the following morning. One hour before leaving Castelnuovo, I had met Elizabeth, only for a brief moment, trying vainly once more to persuade her to follow us but she could not leave her mother. A few years ago I found her name in the book which confirmed her tragic destiny, together with that of all other Jewish people interned at Castelnuovo. That would have been our destiny too.

We were on the run. We walked in silence, never turning round to catch a last glimpse of Castelnuovo. We were escaping away from the horror of likely death but rushing towards the unknown.

Four hours later we located the river crossing. Once across, we climbed through the woods. At sunset we finally came to a shepherd's hut. It was raining hard. The roof was not watertight but the rain did not bother us. We curled up on makeshift beds of hay and chestnut leaves, preoccupied with only one thought: survival.

The next morning we continued our climb, eventually reaching a small settlement, Colle Panestra. We explained that we had been evacuated from a heavily bombed nearby town and were seeking refuge. We had no documents and no money except for our last ration books from Castelnuovo, on which I had altered 'Kienwald' to 'Rinaldo', since our foreign surname could raise suspicions.

One of the local families, based near Fontana Grande in Lower Piritano, offered us hospitality. At that time all I knew about our location was that we were somewhere on the Alpe di San Antonio. My parents were given a room in the house. My brother and I were told to stay in a nearby forest hut, used to store dry chestnut leaves, and we were given an oil lamp and two blankets. We dug beds into the leaves and wrapped ourselves up in the blankets. We could hear the wind whistling through the walls; it was December, but those makeshift beds were warm.

Tears well up in my eyes when I think of those people's generosity but we could not take advantage of their hospitality for long. We found an uninhabited house at Pasquigliora, not far from Colle Panestra. It belonged to a shepherd from Versilia. There were no mattresses, pillows or blankets but it was dry and safe.

The warden of the mountain refuge Rossi, situated under Pania della Croce, lived in Upper Pirano. He offered to go up to the refuge with us boys to find what we needed. That trek was a nightmare. We had no suitable footwear and we were walking in frozen snow. I did not manage to reach the refuge because the snow crystals had made me dizzy. I waited for the warden to return with my brother, both carrying huge bundles of basic necessities. I relieved them of some of the load and we started our descent.

I lost my footing on the snow and I started to slide downhill. I managed to stop my fall, with the help of some huge boulders, but the seat of my trousers had disintegrated. We made it back to the house with enough bedding for all four of us. I recall a large kitchen downstairs with a fireplace, pots and pans and some other basic household appliances. My brother and I had to collect twigs and small branches.

We learnt to carry heavy loads on our back using a small padded ring over our head. In the winter, wood for the fire was almost more important than food. We worked for the local farmers in exchange for chestnut flour and occasionally an egg or two but, essentially, our diet was based on chestnuts.

I had time to reminisce about the events of the last three years of my life, since that fateful day in June 1940 when we were arrested and sent to the concentration camp of Ferramonti di Tarsia, in the Crati valley, about 30 km from Cosenza.

Then on 4 November 1941 we were sent to Castelnuovo together with several other Jewish families, totalling about 80 people. I only stayed for a few months as miraculously I was given a special permit to complete my studies at a college in Padua. I was 20 years old at that time. I returned to Castelnuovo on 8 September 1943, when German troops entered Padua.

Life in this small foothill town was relatively peaceful until then. When we left to go on the run, we could not take our belongings, not even a change of underwear. It was winter and all our woollen clothing had been locked up in a trunk in the house we occupied in Castelnuovo.

· Somehow my father made contact with a friendly local, who brought the trunk up to Pasquigliora on the back of a mule. My father gave him part of the contents as payment. And so, we continued to survive in that hut, at an altitude of about 1000m.

Our main daily preoccupation was to procure some food and wood for the fire. My brother was four years younger than me and was always hungry. The local farmers were generous and chestnut flour was aplenty. We learnt to make polenta in a copper pot, to pour it on a wooden block and to cut it with a string. We did not wish to be beggars. We did really hard work for them, the worst of which was loading baskets of manure on our back and spreading it on the fields.

In the evening it was just as hard to wash oneself thoroughly to get rid of the smell. Months went by, the winter turned into spring. I did not know about Auschwitz but something was telling me that my family and I had just avoided a terrible fate. It was difficult to live like hunted game in such harsh conditions but looking back today I can say that it was not so bad. It was good to be free and surrounded by nature. We had not lost our dignity, or our identity. We did not know what our end would be but we were living to survive.

In the spring of 1944, Pasquigliora was a war zone. The Gothic Line was a few hundred metres away. A dirt road half way up Mount Piglionico led to the foot of Pania della Croce. There, at a place called the Rocchette, was our ticket to freedom, the gateway to no-man's land.

A small group of partisans, known as 'Il Gruppo Valanga', led by Leandro Puccetti was operating on Monte Rovaio. We helped them to recover supplies dropped by allied planes. Summer was approaching and almost every day formations of bombers were flying overhead. One morning a bomb landed in the area of Fontana Grande and made us feel as if we were directly involved in the conflict. There were other similar episodes: the unexpected encounter between my father and I and a group of fascist paramilitaries who were asking whether we had seen any partisans in the area; the dialogue near Fontana Grande with an unarmed German soldier who was trying to abscond and one day, when I was approaching the local teacher's house, I heard two German SS suggesting to each other that they might like to shave my beard off (although I spoke perfect German, I feigned not to understand what they were saying).

On 29 August 1944 we were woken up by a tremendous exchange of fire not far from us. I looked out of the window, it was still dark but the night was lit by tracer bullets being fired in all directions. It appeared that we were surrounded. We dressed quickly and left the house, descending towards the stream, thinking that we would be safer below the level of the bullets. We followed the stream towards the mill. We had heard from the miller that he had dug a shelter in the woods. He welcomed us and several other men who were seeking refuge, including the young local priest. While the women felt that they were safe outside, 12 men crawled into the shelter and lay there one next to the other for three days and three nights. The women brought us some pasta from time to time.

On that occasion, I had the opportunity of witnessing my mother's courage; she was a shy and slender-built woman but she dared to try to salvage a few things from our hut and came face to face with some SS. The Germans were torching every house. The partisans were fighting hard but twenty men fell and the others ran for their lives, sometimes jumping from very high rocks. Leandro Puccetti was mortally wounded in the process. On day four, with the German troops having left the area, two men came to our shelter asking for help. Two of us climbed through the woods towards Case Tievora and we reached Fontana Guidone where we found Puccetti near death. We sat him on a chair and lifted it with two long poles so that four of us could carry him downhill to the teacher's house, the only one still standing since it was brick built. We laid him on a bed. He was blue. I heard later that some partisans managed to take him under a false name to the hospital in Castelnuovo where he died a few days later.

Now we were really on our own. Our house, and all the other houses were burned to the ground. Most of the local people had left and those few who had stayed behind were living in fear. We had lost everything and did not know where to go next. We climbed back up to Monte Panestra and followed a steep footpath at the back of a burned-out ruin. We found a large cave that had been used to store hay. This became our lodging until the end of November.

Today I often wonder how we managed to survive there. Every moment of every day all we could think of was how to get out of this terrible situation. Winter was approaching. I decided to seek help from a large partisan group, led by a British major, which was operating on the opposite slope of the Turrite. Following the directions given to me by a shepherd who acted as my guide for part of the way, I descended from Monte Rovaio, crossed the valley and climbed up the other side. It was an interminable and exhausting walk but I finally met Major Oldham, to whom I provided information about the Rocchette and the position of the American V Army. He promised that he would send a man to accompany us across the front line. I returned to our cave, days passed by and nothing happened. From our position and without binoculars I could see the Rocchette and men moving about up there but I could not tell who they were. The wait was becoming unbearable and every day that passed was making our situation worse. One morning my father and I finally concluded that we had no other choice but to try and cross the line, fully aware that the risks were stacked against us. We started our walk and we reached the road immediately below the Rocchette.

The mountain was shrouded in fog that morning and therefore we were startled when three soldiers suddenly emerged from the cotton-wool-like cloud. They were wearing the helmet of the *bersaglieri*. It was not looking good. One of the soldiers shouted, "Jews!"

We were lost. He repeated, "I know them. They are Jews." It was only after a few more seconds that they threw down their helmets and revealed themselves as partisans who had been wearing the uniforms of some Italian prisoners they had captured. We embraced them. We asked them whether they thought it would be possible for us to cross the front line. They believed that there was only a small window of opportunity but that they would not be able to hold the position for very much longer. With great courage and daring, the four of us together with a local woman shepherding about 30 sheep ventured up to the Rocchette. By the time we reached the pass, an intense exchange of fire was taking place but it was too late to go back or to find shelter.

We ran downhill until we were well away from the site of the battle. We were in no-man's land and stopped at a small village where we slept on the floor of an empty house. It was 22 November 1944. The next morning we were on our feet once again but we were overcome with emotion when we met an American patrol, who gave us some chocolate and took us to their camp. My father tore off his coat's epaulet and produced his old Polish passport. They took us to Gallicano, moving away from the front line, and then to Viareggio.

It was not paradise. All hotels and guesthouses were devastated. We slept on floors and we were even more starved than on the Alpe. A bowl of soup provided daily by the Americans was not enough. But we had survived the nightmare and this was giving us strength. After a few days we were introduced to a Jewish officer who took us by jeep to Lucca. Finally the authorities took note of us and we were given proper accommodation.

This is the end of our little odyssey, which was wonderful when compared with what it might have been without my small act of daring, the result I am sure of the flicker of *Hashgacha Pratis* which guides all of us Jews. After all, notwithstanding 'the final solution', I am here with children and grandchildren and my brother is a Rabbi in Bnei Brak, with a son and many grandchildren.

I have told this story so that its memory should not be lost.

Leonardo Kienwald

I am overcome with emotion every time I read this story and, although this is only one of thousands of similar narratives, it is unique because of where it took place. Considering that my father and his family were the only survivors of all the Jews of Castelnuovo di Garfagnana, I owe it to his blessed memory that his story should be published.

Dr Eli Kienwald, London

My Grandparents, Oskar and Rachel

My mother, Celeste di Segni

My father, Leonardo Kienwald

Oskar Kienwald's business card

Zew Kutten

I do not remember Ferramonti. I remember stories, photographs, opinions. My parents, Polish Jews, fled from Poland to Slovakia crossing the Tatra mountains and they boarded the "ship" Pentcho that would take them to Israel (then Palestine). After months of adventures (delays, mined waters, wrecked ship) they arrived in Rhodes where I was born. Everyone on the Pentcho was eventually transferred to Ferramonti, both detention and salvation camp. The fate of the Jews (including my family's) in the German and Polish camps is well known. Same for the Sephardic communities in Rhodes.

The story about Ferramonti includes confinement, work, good treatment, food rationing and restricted communications with outside. The confinement was relative, you could walk around, exchange products for services with neighbours. The food was not abundant, but at least there was something. I include a photo with my parents: they are thin and I was well fed. I believe I was raised on condensed milk (that must be the reason why I now prefer condensed milk to any marmalade). You could receive "letters" from abroad: they were open letters on Red Cross forms with a maximum of 25 words. They were very moving: "live with hope," one said. It was painful when they stopped coming. You could guess the reasons.

Something to notice: the commitment of the camp commander towards the inmates' lives. Many times I heard my parents praise them and other similar stories. This makes me think: how many kinds of freedom are there? Live, be confined to live? Today I am not confined but I must restrict my movements because the pandemic forces me to do so. Do I exercise my freedom by choosing a relative confinement? Ferramonti did not allow that choice. The other camps even less. In terms of the treatment (and I highlight this): there are no options in a system that does not give options. Sometimes there are; it is a matter of putting them into play.

Zew Kutten, Buenos Aires

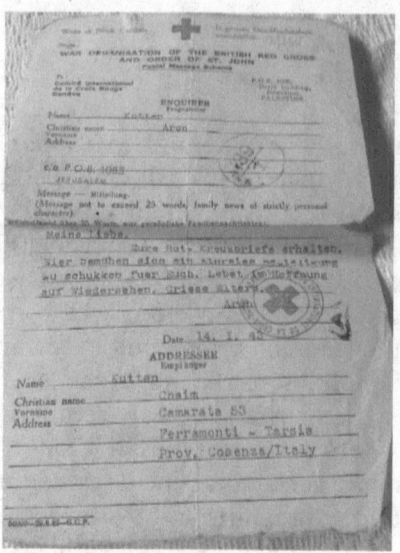

"Live with hope." 14.1.43

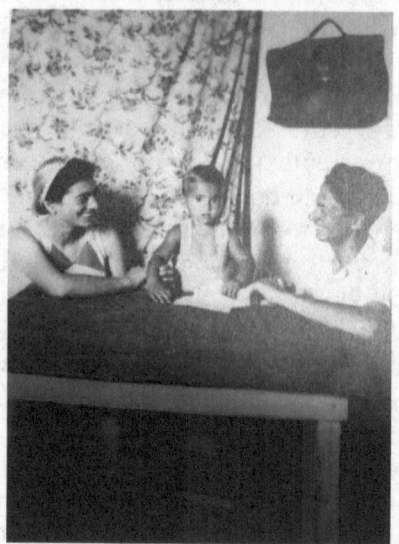

Ferramonti: young Zew with his parents

Ernesto and Anny Lazar

In Our Family's Memory

At home in Rome, within our family, it was normal to hear about the concentration camp of Ferramonti di Tarsia where my parents, Ernesto and Anny Lazar, had been detained from May 1943 until December 1944; since we were children, not only did our parents tell us of their birth city, Vienna, of their escape from Austria towards Zagabria after the Anschluss, and of their forced permanence in Nizza Monferrato; they also would tell us about their captivity in Ferramonti di Tarsia, even before our friend Carlo Spartaco Capogreco had started to write his book, disclosing the history of Ferramonti to the world.

They used to tell us about the humanity shown by their keepers, by part of the management, by the people of Calabria.

My parents arrived in Ferramonti on 11 May 1943 and were married in July, two months before the allied liberation. Until a few years ago they maintained regular contact with the daughters of Fraticelli, the Camp manager after the liberation, and marshal Marrari. For years, together with other ex-internees, they tried to obtain for Fraticelli and Marshal Marrari the recognition of Righteous among Nations (*Chassid Umot Haolam*) by the Institution Yad Vashem in Jerusalem. But although their attempts were consolidated by extensive endorsement, they failed to obtain the result expected; inasmuch as though the Commission in Yad Vashem confirmed that Fraticelli and Marshal Marrari had showed humanity towards the captives, they could not establish that those people's lives had been exposed to major danger and serious risk, which is a prerequisite to be granted that recognition.

Beniamino Lazar, Israel

My father Ernesto Lazar Recalls.....

In Nizza Monferrato we were advised that we would be taken to a camp in Ferramonti, a site near Tarsia. We were in

Calabria. A few detainees, who were helping us to unload our baggage, reassured us by saying that though the camp was built on the German model, it was not like Auschwitz or Dachau, though it was still a concentration camp. While observing their faces and their expressions, we immediately realised that Fraticelli and Marshal Marrari were good people, helpful and kind; even during such a gloomy period they never lost their humanity. However, we were very scared; our future appeared more and more uncertain.

Women and men were housed in separate buildings. First, we queued for registration, then we stood in line and were given sacks we had to fill with straw, blankets and grey sheets riddled with holes, that we arranged on some beds. Each building housed about thirty-six of us. The camp was surrounded by barbed wire and patrolled by armed militia. We were summoned for roll call every morning and evening; we had to respond "present" promptly. Then they would hand us our daily bread ration, while we had to get drinking water from the fountain located in the central area of the camp. Some buildings had toilets installed, and others had washrooms.

My mother Anny Schiff Lazar recalls......

We were about two thousand people in the camp: Jews, anti-fascist Catholics, Protestants, Chinese and many gypsies, a human concoction confined in that unsanitary and swampy place full of mice, bugs, lice, mosquitos and malaria. Actually, in spite of the quinine we took every day, we all caught malaria. We even had a public kosher kitchen, though it only supplied pasta with chickpeas. Those who had some money could buy fruit and other food from the militia. Even farmers used to sell their produce or would barter it for clothes or shoes, from outside the camp.

On 4 July 1943 Ernesto and I got married; our youth, our love and our strength were more powerful than our fear or terror of death; perhaps we wished to challenge fate. It was a poor but moving ceremony. A rabbi from Sussak, Yugoslavia, married us, a tailor from Slovakia made my wedding outfit out of a white sheet; a Chinese man painted my wooden shoes with white paint. I even made a lace hat, and Marshal Marrari gave me some white daisies from his garden to keep up the tradition. There was a large tallit (Jewish ritual shawl) held by four wooden posts under the open sky; the sun shone on this hot July day while all around us the detainees shared our joy.

A little 'reception' followed with potato salad, stale bread, a honey cake my mother made and, as we were in Italy, a bottle of wine that someone gave us could not be missed. This humble reception was appreciated more than a magnificent lunch. I was happy; though I missed my father and all my deported relatives, and Ernesto was worried because he had not had any news about his family for a long time, we hoped for a future full of peace and freedom.

Unfortunately, just a few days after, there was an attack of 'friendly fire' by an allied plane overhead which mistook Ferramonti for a German army base. Machine-gun fire from the low-flying plane strafed the camp causing 4 deaths, including a friend of mine who had celebrated her marriage less than a month before.

Beniamino Lazar, Israel

Ernesto Lazar, Ferramonti 1943

Ernesto Lazar and Anny Schiff, Ferramonti. Wedding day 4.7.1943

Siegfried and Hilda Margoniner

Hilda and Siegfried Margoniner boarded the train at Willhelmshafen, once the main North Sea port of the German Imperial Navy, on the 10th of April 1934. They left behind the city in which they had spent their married life and built the well-known Margoniner department store. They headed south, to Rome via Vienna, hoping that the German people would soon come to their senses and expel Herr Hitler and his Nazi acolytes.

Young Bernhard (13) happily boarded the train with his parents and left behind the constant bullying that he had been subjected to by his anti-Semitic classmates. His older sister Inge had left a few weeks earlier for Berlin, after being barred from attending school, to train as a dental technician. She would join them later in Rome and add her meagre income to that of Bernhard's running errands in a photo shop, and renting out a few rooms with board.

These were difficult times, but they were happy that they had managed to escape the Nazis and full of hope once the longed-for tourist visa to Uruguay arrived. Inge and Bernhard boarded the last passenger ship that left Genoa for Uruguay before the war. The plan had been that Inge and Bernhard would settle down and prepare the ground for their parents' arrival after a few months. However, the well laid plan did not materialize because the war in Europe broke out. After boarding the ship there was no more contact between the parents in Italy and the children in Uruguay and it would be re-established only after five long years.

Siegfried had suffered from a weak heart for some time and in the meantime, realized that under the present circumstances, his days were numbered and wrote a touching farewell letter to Hilde.

In Rome the situation of the "ebrei stranieri" (foreign Jews) deteriorated steadily, and after being incarcerated for some time, in early July 1940 Siegfried was transferred to the concentration camp at Ferramonti and Hilda to *confino libero* in

Lanciano. Siegfried passed away on 11th July 1940 shortly after his arrival at Ferramonti and was buried on July 17th where his grave is one of only 4 remaining Jewish graves in the Catholic cemetery in Tarsia a few kilometres from Ferramonti camp.

Hilda spent more than three years in Lanciano, an "open camp" in the Abruzzi. After the liberation she made her way to Artessa and met Joseph (Jupp) Meyer, whom she would marry before boarding the USS "Henry Gibbons". This ship conveyed to the US close to 1,000 Jews specially selected by a committee led by Ruth Gruber, the famous photographer turned General*. The US had steadfastly refused to accept immigrants during the war, but a special dispensation issued by President F. D. Roosevelt allowed 1,000 displaced persons to temporarily live in the US until the war was over. Selected from over 3,000 applicants, 982 refugees boarded the transport and sailed from Naples in July 1944. It is not completely clear what the criteria for selection were, but apparently Jupp and Hilda satisfied the members of the committee and they were amongst the chosen few.

Once the refugees arrived in the US on the 3rd August 1944, they were transferred to the Fort Ontario Emergency Refugee Shelter in Oswego, NY. It was strange for the refugees to find themselves once again behind barbed wire, but after a short while they established friendly relations with the local population. Hilda worked as a therapeutic masseuse in Newark, and Jupp found work in a nearby fertilizer factory.

After arriving in the US Hilda tried to locate her children in South America. She managed to establish contact with them thanks to the Red Cross. In 1945, she proudly announced in "Aufbau," the local newspaper published by the German-speaking Jewish community, the marriage of her son Bernhard, now aged 24, and Margot in Montevideo.

Refugees who could travel to relatives in other countries, were not allowed to stay in the US after the war. A few months after locating her children and soon after Bernhard's wedding in 1945, Hilda persuaded the captain of a cargo boat travelling

---

* cf. https://www.timesofisrael.com/the-woman-who-launched-1000-jewish-refugees

to South America to take her along. He agreed, but being the sole female on board, she spent the entire trip hidden in his cabin. Three months later Joseph followed her to Uruguay. They rented a small shop in Montevideo and made their home in the shop's basement.

Montevideo, the capital of Uruguay, was a small city, particularly when compared to pre-war Berlin. Inge could not work as a dental technician and her work as an au-pair, posing as an Englishwoman or at least educated in Great Britain, did not satisfy her. She decided to try her luck in Buenos Aires, the Paris of South America and capital of Argentina. In 1941 she was rowed across the Uruguay River, the natural boundary between the two countries, and made her way to Buenos Aires.

The German Jew expatriates were a relatively close-knit community and led a lively social life. In one of the meetings Inge met Werner Berliner. He had left his native Frankfurt in 1937, directly for Buenos Aires. When they met, rumors of the liquidation of European Jewry had started to reach them. Following a relatively long courtship Inge married Werner on D-Day, 6 June 1944, choosing a black dress to signify the unknown fate of her parents. They had two children, Peter (1946-) and Freddy (1950-1979). Freddy, a journalist and a political activist, was captured by one of the security branches of the fascist government then in power, brutally tortured and killed. Peter moved to Israel in 1970, married Kelly (1948-2014), had three children and to date, seven grandchildren. Kelly was a dedicated and beloved elementary school teacher and Peter pursued a successful academic career in the field of water use in agriculture.

Epilogue

Bernhard and Margot met soon after his arrival in Montevideo in 1939. They married in 1945 and had two children: Susy (1951) and Rudy (1953).

Rudi married Gaby and became a successful architect establishing building companies both in his home country, Uruguay, and in Chicago (U.S.A.). They have one son, Adrian, also an architect, and a grandson, Alexander Margoniner.

Susy, mother of Silvana and Diego, and grandmother of a boy and a girl, became a teacher of English and opened her own school with close contacts with the U.K. In 2017 during an annual visit to England with her students, she met Yolanda Ropschitz-Bentham, (editor of this publication), who had noticed Siegfried's grave in Tarsia cemetery and tracked the family down via Facebook.

Jupp, Hilda's second husband, passed away in 1962, Bernhard in October 1981 and Inge in March 1982. Hilda, the tough survivor of persecution, concentration camps and emigrations passed away on the 19th Oct 1986 at the age of 91.

Pedro Berliner, Israel

Siegfried in Italy

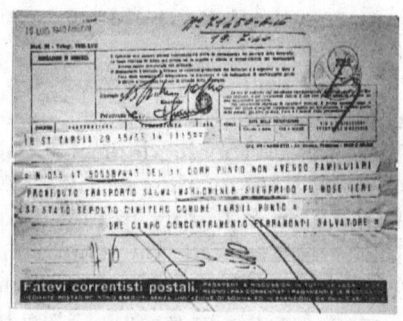

Telegram informing of burial of Siegfried Margoniner in Tarsia cemetery, signed by Paolo Salvatore, Camp Director, Ferramonti

Hilda and Siegfried in Rome

Hilda Margoniner

Rom den 6.April 1940.

Mein Vermaechtnis

dem liebsten und besten Menschen auf der Welt,mit dem
ich Freud und Leid waehrend vierundzwanzig Jahre teilte

meiner H I L D A

Jnnigstgeliebte,
wenn Du diesen Brief nach meinem Tode
findest,hat unser Glueck ein Ende fuer immer!Wir haben
mit unseren beiden Kindern-Jnge und Bernhard-schoene,
sehr schoene Zeiten verlebt,allerdings auch sorgenvolle
Tage und Jahre durchgemacht,aber wo Sonne ist,kommt ab
und zu auch mal Schatten.Doch nichts,garnichts hat je
unsere Eintracht,unser Zusammenleben gestoert und einer
lebte fuer den anderen.Was Du mir aber in all den Jahren
gewesen bist,mein Kind,weiss nur ein Gott!Auf der ganzen
Welt gibt es nicht eine Frau,die waehrend ihrer Ehe dem
Mann mehr Liebe,Mitempfinden und Guete gegeben hat wie
Du mir und dafuer sei Dir gedankt,tausendmal innigst
gedankt.Wenn ich ferner bedenke,wie Du unsere geliebten,
fern von uns jetzt weilenden Kinder erzogen und zu bra-
ven,tuechtigen Menschen gemacht hast,so steht Dir auch
dafuer mein innigster Dank zu!Nicht vergessen moechte
ich an die ueberaus grosse Liebe all meinen Geschwistern
und Verwandten gegenueber und ich kenne keinen in der
Familie,der Dich nicht zu seinen Freunden zaehlt.
So habe ich nur einen Wunsch,mein Engel und zwar,dass Du
bald,sehr bald mit unseren Kindern vereint wirst,was mir
ja leider versagt blieb!Graeme Dich nicht zu sehr ueber
meinen Tod,denn zuerst sorge dafuer,dass Du gesund blei-
ben wirst!Meine letzten Jahre waren viel durch Krankhei-
ten gestoert,doch Du und unsere Kinder gaben mir stets
Mut und neue Kraft!Jetzt ist alles vorbei,behalte mich
weiter in gutem Gedenken,denn ich bin bis zum letzten
Atemzug Deiner Kinder's Vater und Dein

Sieg

Siegfried's letter to Hilda (Translation below)

Rome 6th of April 1940

My bequest/legacy

To the best and most beloved person in the world, with whom I shared sorrow and joy during twenty four years,

My Hilda,

My very beloved, when you will find this letter after my death, our happiness will have ended forever. We had, with our two children, Inge and Bernhard, nice, very nice times, even though there were days and years full of worry, but wherever the sun shines there are sometimes shadows. But never ever did anything affect or interfere with the harmony of our companionship, our living for each other. What you were for me during all these years my child, only the Gods know. There is not another woman on the whole world who throughout her marriage granted her husband more love, empathy, and kindness than you granted me and therefore you should be thanked, thanked a thousand times from the depth of my heart. Furthermore, if I reflect on how you educated our dear and now far away children to be serious, hardworking persons, I have to thank you for that as well from the bottom of my heart. I do not want to forget your love for all my sisters and relatives, and I do not know anybody in our family that does not count you among their friends.

I have only one wish my angel, and that is that soon, very soon you will be reunited with our children, something which I will unfortunately not be able to do. Do not mourn too much for my death and take good care of your health. My last years were fettered by my illness, but you and the children supported me always and infused me with courage and energy. Now that everything has ended, keep me in your thoughts, because I am till my last breath the father of your children and your

Sieg

Richard and Hella Mayer

Richard and Helena Mayer and daughter Miriam

I, Miriam, daughter of Richard Mayer, was born in Novi Sad, former Yugoslavia, now Serbia in 1939. The war against Yugoslavia started in April 1941 and my parents and I fled from Novisad, in April, came back, were there during the massacre of January 1942 and were lucky to escape to Budapest then Zagreb. We got false passports, pretending to be Aryans, my father being blue-eyed and named Richard Mayer, a good German name, that helped us fly to Venice on a Lufthansa flight (real *chutzpa* as my father used to say) in December 1942. My father was imprisoned in Venice and then the three of us were deported to Ferramonti on December 26, 1942.

My father was arrested as a "political prisoner", probably because of the false passports. During his prison time my mother contacted a Jewish lawyer in Venice, who advised them to reveal our Jewish identity and so we got transported to Ferramonti. As for me, they wanted to put me with some nuns and imprison my mother too, but she refused to be parted from me, so the Italians being Italians, put the two of us in a hotel instead. Luck was on our side, for sure. This comes out in my father's memoirs all the time.

Richard Mayer tells the story

......Finally we arrived in Cosenza, the capital town of the district of Calabria. We had to proceed to Ferramonti by bus, but an official in Cosenza told us, "There is no hurry to arrive in Ferramonti. I will take care of your hotel, and you enjoy Cosenza for a few days, being Christmas time anyhow." The man knew what he was talking about. After having had a good time in Cosenza, our arrival in Ferramonti gave us a real shock. We arrived there in a rickety bus, pressed among a crowd of shouting, wildly gesticulating peasants, while it was raining desperately the whole time.

The first impression of the camp was of long lines of wooden barracks in a sea of mud. In the entrance were two guards, and inside the camp, the first resident we saw looked like an old tramp, a man covered with sacks and shivering in the cold. Our luggage on the top of the bus was a real mess from all that rain. Hella wept heavy tears; I became very angry indeed, and even our little girl didn't like the place. In the office, near the entrance, our agents handed us over to the camp authorities. We got some straw mattresses, and we were shown to our new residence, where we were to live for almost a year. After the good days of Venice and San Donna di Piave and transit via Rome to Cosenza, we felt very unhappy indeed. Families with children had the privilege of one small room for themselves divided from the second room by a shared kitchen, where another family lived. Single people were in common barracks for 30–40 people each, and married people who had no children also had to stay in the common barracks but were separated because there were barracks only for men and barracks only for women. Thanks to our daughter we had the good luck to come to such luxury accommodation — in comparison to the common barracks. It seems all is relative in life.

Next morning when the sun came out in its splendid glory, matters seemed somewhat friendlier. The partners of our housing unit were Italian Jews, the missus singing the whole day the newest Italian hits, singing strictly through her nose but with much emotion. At a later date an Austrian family came in to the second room of our unit. They had a blonde grown up daughter with no good reputation as for her morals. The main attraction of our household was Mr Lancet, whom we inherited from the previous tenant of our room. Lancet, a young Slovak Jew, a butcher by profession, was our all-round man. He was our cook, butler, chambermaid, baby sitter, public relations man, our go-between to the black marketeers for providing food, and killer of bugs, which lovely little insects we had in masses. Without Lancet, life wouldn't have been so easy in Ferramonti.

(When he came to Israel, he married a medical doctor in Tel Aviv.)

We made a lot of friends in the shortest time and maintained an open house—or, better, open room. It is said Tel Aviv is a little New York, and if this is correct, so was Ferramonti a caricature of Tel Aviv. Quite the same mixture of people as in Israel—Jews from all over the world—only the government, respectively the management, was much better than in Israel, so under given poor circumstances everything worked satisfactorily. In no time we had coffee houses, orchestras, schools, ballet lessons, lectures, synagogues (for all the trends), a bath house, merchants—rather, black marketeers, tenors and baritones, dentists, and even a supermarket. It's true that mostly nothing else could be purchased there apart from cauliflower. The manager, Mr Baum, a Yugoslav, when asked what he is selling today, would point proudly to his buttonhole, where he had a blossom of cauliflower fixed. Ours was such a wild green cauliflower, but the Jewish genius developed a whole range of dishes made of green cauliflower, from Beef Stroganoff to all kinds of fancy cakes. After Ferramonti I couldn't look at cauliflower for years.

With plenty of free time, there were new daily scandals to be discussed—whose wife had been caught with whom, etc. Best proof that it wasn't as bad as that in concentration camp Ferramonti di Tarsia. We had also our minorities. We had Yugoslav partisans for making from time to time some communist demonstrations, Chinamen who took care of the laundry, converted Jews to carry a big cross in religious processions, and English and Frenchmen for having also some distinguished people around. Except that we were counted daily—for checking that we are still there—we did not feel much the presence of our Italian hosts, although the guards and the management as well were all militia men, the equivalent of the German S.S. Nevertheless, all of them were more or less quite kind human beings.

It was strictly forbidden to leave the barracks after 8 p.m. In spite of that, there was traffic from barrack to barrack also at night time. One night I walked down the main street of the camp in full moonlight when a single dark-skinned militia man approached me in a menacing manner. It wasn't so agreeable, and I thought here I am in big trouble. He looked right, he looked left, he looked behind himself, and he whispered like a conspirator out of a cheap opera, "You want to buy cheese, Sir?" and when I looked astonished or perhaps still afraid, he said, "Don't be afraid, Sir, it's not expensive. I make it for you a real bargain," and out came from under the militia pelerine a wonderful round ball of caciocavallo cheese. Everything was organized thoroughly, so the black marketeers had a fixed price to pay to the Italian entrance guard for every sack of goods smuggled into the camp. Of course, one tried to cheat the other. When one of the smugglers did not pay the established customs charge correctly, the guard followed him to his barrack, leaving his rifle at the gate. "You son of a bitch, you cheated me! You paid only for two sacks, but I am not blind, you carried three sacks." The smuggler paid the difference honourably.

We often entertained our friends in the evenings during curfew times, and there were sometimes quite noisy parties. After such a party I was summoned by our camp director, a militia major, and he told me, "There was light to be seen from your window. Your blackout was not in order. So I looked for a long time through your window. You had such a good time that I would have loved to join the party. Remember that for next time."

At that time Hella became aware that she is really born to be a playwright and stage manager. So she sat down one morning and rewrote the stories of Snow White and the Seven Dwarfs and Cinderella into theatre plays for children. I appreciate it very highly even today that she did not cast the leading parts to our daughter. Modesty this way or modesty that way, you can be assured that our little daughter had been richly compensated. She had a solo dance in the show. It was some kind of Oriental dance to the music of the Persian Market, and she did it in a yellow robe. I never understood why it had to be yellow when there was no yellow cloth available in Ferramonti. But a stage manager should know better, and so Hella took great pains to dye a white fabric yellow with Atebrin. I suppose that thanks to Atebrin (anti-malarial drug) the dance of our daughter became a great success. She had no stage fright and when the show was over, she asked most intelligently, "When will I have to dance for the real performance?" She thought it was just another rehearsal.

On the subject of Atebrin: Ferramonti was a malaria area, and we had to take our daily ration of Atebrin. Astrid and I escaped it, but Hella got it badly and was ill for a long time.

We had also a more serious plague. The Germans called for us on several occasions, but as it was said, Mussolini insisted we were his Jews, and so we were spared to be burned in Auschwitz. From day to day the war came nearer to Ferramonti. For weeks the Allied bomber formations flew over our heads to the north, and after they dropped their bombs, they came the same way over our heads back to their bases, probably in Sicily, which was already in Allied hands. It became routine, and we knew exactly the hour and even the minutes when they flew to action and again back to base. We greeted the pilots emotionally and stretched our necks skywards as long as we could see them. It was a part of our daily routine.

One day on the way back from action, one of the planes came down to a very low altitude right over our heads and machine-gunned the camp, the result being five dead and I do not remember how many wounded. It must have been a novice who probably thought we were some German army base. But even such dramatic events have also their comic aspects. A Yugoslav acquaintance of ours happened to be at the time of the machine-gunning in a public W.C., the only brick construction in the camp, the other buildings being wooden. A long time after the air raid somebody wanted to enter the W.C.; after waiting and waiting and the door was still closed, he started to bang on the door until a hysterical voice quivered out of the W.C., "What a disregard, when human life is in question. You should be ashamed," and he did not open the door. He survived and later became a professional Zionist in Israel but had a change of heart and returned to Yugoslavia as an ardent communist.

We had a new enjoyment in the camp. For weeks we could see on the nearby high-road the German army in retreat northwards. I would observe them through my window night after night. It was for me the sweetest sight I ever saw.

Although they still marched in perfect formations, it seemed to us to be the beginning of the end. With the advance of the Allies, the front came nearer to us each day, and when shooting started around our camp, we decided it was time to get out.

Nobody from the Italian management was to be found. They had probably run away a while before, and we had not for long to persuade the guards to open the gates and to let us out. In fright they joined us willingly, and we ran all together in all directions a fast as we could. Quite easy to understand. Who wants to be the target in the middle of two shooting enemies, especially when the shooting became louder and louder, and we couldn't do anything about it? We made it to the nearby mountains, all the time Allied airplanes zooming over our heads. We arrived at the first village on top of the mountain to find the peasants in hot panic, the women folk running around and shouting hysterically for the help of Jesus, Maria, and all the saints. Our Allies behaved tip-top; they did not drop a single bomb and after a while finally disappeared. We found a kind of stable to make us feel comfortable after all that running. Maybe it was not quite a stable, but we shared it with chickens, goats, and a few pigs day and night. The first constructive step we did, to celebrate the advance of the Allies, was that we bought a beauty of a calf in partnership with a few families. Our Mr Lancet, a trained butcher and cook, took care of it so that this calf was transformed to delicious roast, schnitzel, and goulash. Thus we celebrated in style, and beside that we were rather starved after all that Ferramonti cauliflower diet. Since our stable partners did not allow us too much sleep, we instead admired big fires blasting on all surrounding mountaintops as a sign that the war in Italy was over.

Our stable domicile was also a remarkable place insofar as our daughter got her first, and I think last, beating from her mother. She felt so happy in the stable, after the delight of the unaccustomed schnitzel, that she threw a pack of special small playing cards to the wind to play with them and in all directions to the chickens and goats. Astrid retaliated successfully without delay. She developed jaundice, and consequently we now felt unhappy. Since the shootings and bombings stopped very soon, we went back to our camp. Next day we enthusiastically welcomed the entry of American and British troops plus the Jewish Brigade to Ferramonti. We were free people again.

Miriam takes up the story again

After liberation we were taken to a camp in El Shatt, Egypt, and since we had visas for Palestine (sent to us from my grandparents who were already in Jerusalem), made it to Jerusalem on May 14th 1944.

Our lives there started as new immigrants; I went to Kindergarten and my parents struggled to make ends meet. We lived through the War of Independence and the establishment of the State of Israel. I completed my schooling, served in the Israeli army, attended the Hebrew University and married an Israeli in 1962. We went through the Six Day War, the Yom Kippur War and all the unsettled times in-between.

My father worked for the British until the establishment of the State of Israel and then joined my grandfather in an agency representing a Dutch firm importing raw materials for the Enamel and Pottery industry in Israel.

My mother had various jobs, taking care of children, sewing leather gloves and then later volunteering in Army prisons.

My husband, being a scientist, had his Post Doc and several Sabbaticals in the USA. We moved to Bethesda Md. in 1977, and this is where we are today.

We have three sons and six grandchildren. My parents passed away in Jerusalem, my father in 1993, my mother in 2010.

Miriam (Astrid) Gery, USA

Ferramonti. Miriam front row, fourth on right

Ferramonti, Comandante Paolo Salvatore in uniform

Miriam in the show produced by her mother

Richard, Miriam and Hella Mayer in their Ferramonti living quarters

Hella and Richard Mayer in their 90s

Miriam (Astrid) today

Zvi Neumann and Gita Friedmann

I would like to dedicate these words to the members of my family who were murdered in the Holocaust, to those who have died, to my dear parents Zvi and Gita, of blessed memory, and to all the non-Jews, wherever they may be, who came to the assistance of my relatives during those difficult years.
Dina Smadar, daughter.

My family's story can be divided into four parts. My mother and her family's flight from Berlin, my father's flight from Slovakia, life in Ferramonti Camp and their *aliyah* (immigration) to Israel where they established a family.

Mother, Gita Friedmann

Berlin, 1933: my mother is 9 or 10 years old.

Around the radio, my grandfather Yehoshua Friedmann, neighbours and friends who did not have their own radio, are gathered and listening tensely. The announcer declares that Hitler has come to power. It is clear to everyone that anti-Semitism will now intensify. The tension is great. Outside, the terrifying sound of goose-stepping boots is heard. Many residents of the neighbourhood have become Nazis; support for the National Socialist party is increasing, even the neighbour across the street... The family is terrified. My grandfather and grandmother were experiencing difficult times and needed to make fateful decisions.

My grandfather wanted to go to Palestine but the limits on immigration were very strict. Immigrants were required to be either affluent, work in an in-demand profession or be farmers. My grandfather was not wealthy; he was an accountant, which was not an in-demand profession in Palestine. My mother would tell how it broke her heart to see his hands covered in the rash he got while learning to be a painter, a profession in demand in Palestine.

Meanwhile, in Berlin, all business with Jews was forbidden, so my grandfather found himself without work.

All the roads were blocked and there was no escape.

"Jews go away," "pig Jews," exclusion, and having our possessions discarded at school became part of our daily routine. The song "When Jewish blood flows from a knife," echoed during school recess. And then my family decided, "Enough!"

My mother asked my grandfather if she could transfer to the school that had been established for Jewish children in converted synagogue offices. Many limitations were placed on the movement of Jews and this severely affected their daily lives.

1938 – There were warnings to return home quickly because of encroaching danger. Synagogues were burning, Jewish-owned stores and businesses smashed and Jewish schools closed. My mother was an eyewitness to Kristallnacht.

The terrifying descriptions can be read in any history book that deals with the period.

"Let's play cards," was a code for transmitting a rumour or information about new decrees or misfortunes. The frequent decrees declared against the Jews did not bypass my family. They were forced to live in a single, sublet room without utensils or property, without even long-term shelter. As a young teenager, my mother was compelled to work in forced labor. Grandfather was taken to the Sachsenhausen camp. He wrote his memoir of the horrors only after immigrating to Israel. He postponed writing and started only after much consideration. In his words, it was very difficult to recount what occurred in the camps, because human language is too poor to describe the tortures and suffering. Very few inmates of Sachsenhausen survived the war. The Jews interned there were denigrated, beaten, starved and suffered many diseases, even before they were sent to the gas chambers.

To be an equal human being among other humans was his only wish.

My mother remembers that during one of the visits permitted in the camp, her father, my grandfather, could not control himself, stepped out of line and kissed her. Immediately, a vile SS officer struck him hard. My mother cried that entire night and even now the stinging pain of those moments has not healed.

My grandfather wrote:

We, the Jews of Berlin, had already heard about Sachsenhausen. We knew it was hell. We were so frightened of the place that we dared not pronounce its name aloud, thinking that its very mention would bring us closer to its gates. But the road there was so horrible that we could not wait to arrive. And then, even after we heard so much about the place and envisioned the worst we could imagine, the reality was insufferable. We went to Sachsenhausen to be tortured and beaten to death. Our tormentors used every means at their disposal to satisfy their sadistic urges: they beat us with their hands and with sticks, pushed us with clenched fists and trampled on us. They would select someone and punch him with their fists until he fell; once he was on the ground, they would step on him. When the victim stood up, they'd push him down again. The game would continue until the miserable victim remained lying on the ground and died in misery. At the beginning, we pitied the dead but within two days, we came to envy them, particularly those who died in transit. They were tortured the least. They beat one because he was married and another because he was single. When the victims cried out in pain, they would be hit again because they dared to scream; but if they held their tongue, the beating continued because they were silent.

We were beaten at all hours of the day; morning, noon and night. We would be summoned outside for a beating. They did not pass up any opportunity; they continually found and created opportunities. They could do whatever they wanted to us. Every one of them would beat us. Once it would be SS soldiers or "the bloc leaders," and another time, SS soldiers who were in a camp because they'd committed some offence. The prisoners who served as "bloc supervisors" also beat us. Once the supervisor in our bloc did not know how to give a beating. Therefore, he was relieved of his duties after five days and assigned to a group sentenced to punitive labor. His successor did know how give a beating and he was the worst of all.

For entire days, we were forced to lie on the floor with our hands behind our backs. We lay in a puddle of perspiration and were so thirsty that we lapped our own sweat off the dirty floor. Many were jealous of my sleeping place beneath a window be-

cause at night I could lick the accumulated moisture off the window panes. We lost our sense of disgust. We saw only liquid, even if it was only salty sweat. I know that anyone who did not experience this torture personally cannot possibly understand how people who valued aesthetics and hygiene could sink so low but we were no longer human. We were nothing more than crushed, dehydrated, tortured, creatures who wanted to drink something, no matter what.

During this period, we could not eat bread because there was no moisture in our mouths to chew it. When we did try to eat bread with dry mouths, it stuck to the roof of our mouths and we had to scrape it away with our fingernails.

Hitler gave instructions that Jews might be released and allowed to leave Germany within one week, if the required documents were obtained. My grandmother Yehudit attempted to bribe officials to have my grandfather released from camp in any possible way. When the longed-for permit was received, we needed to hurry and leave quickly. Otherwise, he would be returned to the camp.

The tale of fleeing through Yugoslavia is filled with the terror of being caught, travelling from village to village disguised as peasants, sleeping in a different place every night, crowding and fear. At the end of a long, tortuous journey my mother, grandfather and grandmother, arrived at the Ferramonti camp in southern Italy. My mother said: "One day we were travelling by train. After a long time, I suddenly saw something blue and smooth through the window. It was the sea." Up until that day, my mother had never seen the sea.

"When we arrived at the camp, we were surrounded by darkness and heard voices. We were afraid. Everything we had experienced left us very uncertain about future events. What next? Frightened, we disembarked from the train and were brought to cabins. Some people were already housed there."

My mother continued:

We shared two small rooms with a couple we had met in a castle, which was a way-station on our journey. A shared kitchenette, lavatory and shower in the courtyard... The Italians gave us a daily allowance that was sufficient to purchase a small amount of food. We were able to cook for ourselves or purchase prepared food. We were hungry the entire time but conditions in Ferramonti could not be compared to what we had experienced in Germany.

Father

My father, Zvi Neumann, left his parents' home in Slovakia when anti-Semitism was on the rise. He left alone at the age of 17 or 18. Being spat upon, jeered and forbidden to study in the academy, left no room for doubt and he decided to leave for Palestine with some comrades. The events that followed proved how right he was. His father and brothers were killed in Bergen-Belsen and many other family members died or were killed.

At this point comes his adventure on the river boat Pentcho, a tale in its own right. I will try to tell it briefly. There were 514 refugees on the river boat and virtually all of them eventually made it to Ferramonti. In his book, Habaita about the history of the boat and life in Ferramonti, Alexander Citron (later Yehoshua Halevy) wrote: "The boat's function was to transport hundreds of Jews to safe shores, travelling an unmarked route."

"None of the passengers deluded himself about the possibility of a smooth journey. The difficulties, the adventures and the life-threatening dangers were taken into consideration in advance. The small boat, already weak with age, could hardly float on the Danube. It endured storms, shaking and blows."

During the difficult journey, the boat sank when it ran aground on the islet of Chamilo Nisi. All of the passengers reached shore, where they tried to retrieve any remaining parts of the boat that might be useful. In the morning, the survivors were able to see that the rocky islet was desolate and uninhabited. They dispatched a boat to seek help but it did not return. Later, they learned that its passengers were hospitalized in Egypt. After many days, an Italian rescue boat arrived and the survivors were transferred to Rhodes and from there 13 months later, to the Ferramonti camp in Calabria. It was now February 1942.

Most of the passengers survived and reached their homeland four years later. Some had chosen to remain in Rhodes which proved to be a tragic mistake.

The extermination of the Jews had begun even before the boat departed. There was an economic and business boycott, windows were smashed. Skulls were smashed. The older generation remained in Slovakia and awaited its bitter fate. Millions were left behind. The Holocaust hit the Jews of Slovakia exceptionally hard and their extermination began in 1942.

In Ferramonti, everyone tried to live a more or less normal life, opening businesses and trying to earn a living. My grandfather, grandmother and the couple they lived with opened a restaurant. The served the meals in their living room to those people in the camp who had enough money to afford it. They had a random collection of utensils and bought food on the black market. Supplies were smuggled by Italian soldiers who earned large sums this way. They obtained flour, oil and other products. My grandmother cooked on a wood-burning stove and the other tenants served the guests. The cooking was done using dark, green olive oil that emitted a heavy stench when used for frying, which spread far and wide. Ever since, my father, Zvi, hated olive oil.

Water was a problem. There was no running water in the restaurant and it was necessary to bring it from wells in the vicinity. My family expected that their efforts would earn them enough profit to provide them with a financial base for the future but the profits were very small.

They raised a turkey and cooked it but they "profited" nothing more than eating the feet, the neck and perhaps the gizzard. They did not allow themselves more than that and did not even dream of breast meat. They worked very hard.

This was the situation: My father arrived from Slovakia on the Pentcho with a group of young people who were highly motivated and full of energy, while my mother had arrived with her parents from Berlin via Yugoslavia after being pursued, denigrated and released from a camp where only a few got out alive.

After the tribulations, suffering and denigration, the Ferramonti camp seemed like the "Garden of Eden." The Italians treated them well and allowed them to manage their own lives, provided that they did not leave the boundaries of the camp. The survivors always mentioned the guards and managers of the camp favourably. There is no doubt that we survived because of them; we owe them our lives.

The hunger, shortages, fleas and other problems were negligible in comparison with what they had experienced before leaving their countries of origin: all they had seen, all they had heard and the family members taken to the gas chambers. And so, community life began to develop within the boundaries of the Ferramonti camp.

My father had learned carpentry in Slovakia and found a variety of odd jobs. He made deck chairs, arm chairs and anything else people requested. He did not turn down any work. He even made the Ferramonti sandals seen in many photos of those days: some of the wood was taken from a storehouse at the site, strips of cloth were cut from the canvas beds, which were wide enough that a strip could be cut from the center. Tacks were made from coins. Ingenious!

Residents and groups in the camp had arrived separately from across Europe and the "promenade" in Ferramonti was a place where they could stroll and meet people. When my father first caught sight of my mother on the promenade, he told his friends, "I'm going to marry her," and began to court her enthusiastically that very day.

When my grandfather wanted a chicken coop it was obvious that my father would be asked to build it. The coop could have been built in 30 minutes but in order to stay near my mother, he stretched the project out for several days.

My father also took advantage of the ping-pong table in the yard to teach his beloved how to play. He wasted no time and went to my grandfather to ask for her hand. There was little time for romance.

Immediately, they began to discuss the wedding which was held in a cabin in the camp. My father and his friends cleaned the place and washed the floor. White sheets became table cloths and old jam jars were used as glasses. They prepared "coffee" from chicory and cake from ricotta cheese. All of their friends baked cakes. The repast included dates and figs, which were plentiful and inexpensive. There were two other weddings on the same day; they even had a bachelor party.

Everyone took the wedding ceremony and entire event very seriously. My mother wore a suit that a friend sewed from remnants of white cloth, her veil was made of mosquito netting and flowers for the bridal bouquet were picked from nearby fields.

The wedding ceremony was conducted by Rabbi Deutsch, and the Chief Rabbi of Genoa, Rabbi Pacifici sent a certificate attesting to the marriage.

Instead of the customary ritual bath before the wedding, my mother was immersed in the river, which was far from clean. Since the camp was closed, she was accompanied by a security guard who turned his back away from the future bride, so he would not see her undress.

Life for the newlyweds was far from simple. Some of the packages my grandfather had sent from Germany eventually arrived in a roundabout way and my grandmother shared their meagre contents with my parents: "A tablecloth for you, a tablecloth for me. A blanket for you, a blanket for us. A towel for you, a towel for us, since you have a new home." When my parents married, they were allocated a single room with my mother's parents with a blanket hung in the middle for privacy.

The lack of their own place and all of the changes they had endured aroused my parents' desire for a cosy, intimate space and intensified their yearning for togetherness. Anything that could decorate or beautify their corner was happily accepted. Friends exchanged objects and crafts, which made it possible for them to decorate their space and give it an intimate, pleasant feeling.

The cabins had straw roofs and huge fleas fell from the straw. Their bites itched, irritated and became infected. My mother remembered burning candles near holes in the walls, to keep the mosquitoes out. They treated the insect-infested mattresses with kerosene. To their dismay, this did not help and the fleas returned.

I was born approximately one-and-a-half years later in October 1944. Since there was no hospital in the camp, when the contractions began my mother was taken, riding on a donkey, to the maternity hospital in Cosenza.

The difficult stories, against the background of war, the smell of death, and uncertainty about the fate of other relatives — whether they had been killed or were still alive — led the Jews and other survivors to search for points of light, amongst the dark and despair. The few that they found were treasured and cherished.

My parents left Ferramonti in June of 1944. They travelled by ship to Alexandria, Egypt and from there took a train to Palestine.

They went first to Netanya, living with another family in a tiny, old, run-down structure, formerly used as a well. Once the neighbourhood of Tovrok was built at the city's outskirts — designed for new immigrants — they moved there. That's where I grew up, living there until age 13. There were 12 buildings in the neighbourhood, each with four families.

In September of 1948, during the War of Independence, my brother was born.

My father supported his family all his life from his carpentry profession. During those difficult years, he never refused a job, no matter how strenuous it was. He was devoted, dedicated, and responsible. He would take whatever job came his way. My mother was an amazing housewife.

My family experienced a long period of hardship but never complained; they were always satisfied with what they had. I never heard stories about the holocaust; I had a wonderful childhood.

Slowly slowly, my parents improved their living conditions. After Tovrok, we moved to a larger apartment in the centre of town, and after a few years, we moved again, further improving our living standards. My parents enjoyed socialising with friends; they would often entertain at each other's houses. During this period, there were many wars in Israel. My father was a soldier and fought in them.

I received my primary education in Netanya. My parents supported my studies but insisted that I learn something practical, so I studied technical drawing. I served in the army and taught Maths and Physics. I met my husband Yehuda there. Later in life, when I was married with three children, I fulfilled my dream of learning art, and that's been the focus of my energy ever since. Yehuda and I have been happily married all these years.

At the end of their life, my parents lived happily in a protected living facility, and that's where they passed away at a ripe old age. They left two children, (my brother and me) six grandchildren and nine great-grandchildren.
Dina Smadar, Israel.

Yehoshua and Yehudit in deck chairs made in Ferramonti, Gita and fiancé Zvi at the table.

The wedding of Gita and Zvi, Ferramonti, October 1942

Gita and Zvi arrive in Netanya with baby Dina, June 1944

Gita and Zvi, 1996, Israel

Dina Smadar today

Moszek Paserman and Chana Cukier

The Paserman family story: from Poland to Pitigliano and Rome

My parents, Moszek Gdala Paserman and Chana Cukier were born in Poland in 1904. Their fathers were in business: the first, a wine and spirits merchant, in Kielce, a town midway between Warsaw and Krakow, the latter, a tobacco merchant in Warsaw.

My parents married in 1927 and settled in Kielce. A few years later Poland started to feel the effects of the 1929 economic crisis. In 1933 they suffered the loss of their 3 year old daughter from diphtheria. So in 1934 they decided to emigrate to Palestine; on their way they stopped in Genoa, where an uncle, Abraham Strosberg, who had been living there since the turn of the century, gave my father work as an agent for his linen company.

My older brother Davide was born in Genoa in July 1935, and I, Leone in March 1939, shortly before the outbreak of WWII. My aunt, Brucha Cukier, came to Genoa to help my mother with my brother and me but was unable to return to Poland, because of the outbreak of WWII on September 1, 1939. After more than 9 months, on June 10, 1940 Italy too entered the war, joining forces with Germany. Soon after, all foreign national Jewish males, age 18 to 60, were deported to concentration camps; my father was taken to Ferramonti, near Cosenza, in Southern Italy, in an area of malaria, with scarce water and few services, but rich in mosquitos and bugs.

My mother with Davide and I had to leave Genoa and settle on a so-called "free internment" in Montefiascone, near Viterbo, some 100 kilometers north of Rome, where there were other interned families. In December 1940, my father was reunited with us in Montefiascone. We survived thanks to a small stipend given by the Italian authorities and to private French lessons given my aunt Brucha.

In 1941 a new problem arose: Davide was 6 years old and needed to go to school, but the 1938 racial laws prevented Jews attending the same schools as Christians. This was a major blow to our parents, who, being educated people, wanted their son to receive an education and to be taught Italian properly. My father made applications in 1941 and 1942 for Davide to be allowed to simply attend school unregistered but these were turned down.

In 1943 the Montefiascone Municipality had to move the Jews out because the Italian army needed their lodgings. My father asked to be transferred to Pitigliano, a village not too far away, where there was a tiny Jewish Community and an elementary Jewish school.

This time his request was granted and in March 1943 we moved to Pitigliano, where Davide, now nearly 8, finally started school, attended by 8 children, of different ages and levels. Although we were the only foreign Jews in Pitigliano, the Pasermans got to know a few Jewish families in the vicinity such as Prof Manlio Paggi who had three sons of similar ages to Davide and me, and the head of the synagogue, Azeglio Servi, so we did not feel quite so isolated.

In the meantime, in July 1943, the allied troops landed in Sicily and in Rome, Mussolini was arrested; on September 8 the new government signed an armistice with the Allies but German troops invaded and occupied North and Central Italy.

In October there was a mass deportation from Rome to Auschwitz: more than 1000 Jewish people were arrested in one single day, October 16.

This news was a sign that the situation was deteriorating rapidly. One night, towards the end of November, a man by the name of Pietro Felici* came to warn our family of a plan he had overheard in a local bar to arrest us the following morning. He offered us a hiding place in his farm, a few miles away. We left immediately and spent the next 7 months hiding in caves; our parents never went outside until June 1944. Davide and I used to play with the farmer's children. The Felici family and their workers provided us with food.

---

* In 2007, Pietro Felici was awarded the certificate of "Righteous among the Nations" by Yad Vashem of Jerusalem.

After June 1944 the situation became safer; the Allies arrived in Pitigliano and our family could leave the caves and return home.

So we were freed in Pitigliano by the allied forces mid-June 1944; yet the war in Italy wasn't over. In fact, the Nazis occupied all of northern Italy, preventing our return to Genoa which we had been forced to leave 4 years earlier. Life in Pitigliano returned slowly to normality, the school reopened in November and my brother Davide, now 9 years old, and I, resumed our education.

My father wanted us to move to Rome, where there was a fairly large number of former displaced persons, (DPs), Shoah survivors, supported by the American Joint Committee. He eventually found a nice 4-roomed flat in a good area, alongside the river Tevere, owned by a Naval officer stationed in Taranto. So, in March 1945, we all moved to Rome. My parents wanted to enrol their 2 children in the Jewish school but they didn't accept us for a number of reasons:

a) the school was already full,
b) it was already towards the end the school year and
c) we were foreigners!

Actually, relations between the Rome Jewish Community and the foreign Jews, mainly former DPs, were not good at all.

So we were enrolled without difficulty in local schools: my brother in the 4th class in the known Convitto Nazionale, just across the bridge over the river, and I in the 1st class in Guido Alessi school in Via Flaminia, also walking distance from our apartment.

So our new life began. There were Shoah survivors, Ashkenazi Jews, most of them widowed and childless so we were virtually the only children in the whole community. In the beginning, there were two Ashkenazi Batei Haknesset, one more Orthodox following Agudat Israel and a second more Zionist-oriented, following the Mizrahi movement. Since most of the former DPs were looking to emigrate outside of Europe, and managed to obtain visas to the US or to South America or even Australia, over time the Agudat Israel Bet Haknesset merged in the Mizrahi one. I remember in

1946, a large theatre was rented by the AJC for Rosh Hashanah and Yom Kippur services!

Ahead of his Bar Mitzvah, David studied Tanach and Mishnah with a good teacher, a certain rav Lemberg and became Bar Mitzvah in 1948. Some 4 years later, rav Lemberg had already left Rome so I studied with an Israeli, a Mr Borochov, who had come to Italy before the war to study medicine but couldn't complete his studies because of the fascist racial laws and the war. In the meantime our father, thanks to his prior bank experience in Poland, found a job with a stocks and gold dealer and money changer.

In September 1947, my parents bought a smaller 3-room apartment in another part of town but still a middle class neighbourhood; obviously David and I changed schools. When he first arrived in Italy my father had worked for his uncle's linen store so, in anticipation of the Catholic Jubilee year of 1950 and potential Rome tourist trade, my parents opened their own linen shop.

Unfortunately, in 1953, my father developed cancer of the colon, necessitating serious and debilitating surgery. While we hoped for a complete recovery, in the autumn of 1954 a metastasis in his lung was discovered, and that was the death bell for us all; he managed to survive almost another 2 years until June 1956 when he passed away at just 51 years old. In accordance with his last wishes, he was buried in Israel. I was 17 years old and still attending high school while my brother was studying law at La Sapienza, University of Rome. My mother Chana survived 20 more years; she passed away in 1976 and was also buried in Israel, next to her beloved husband.

While my mother continued for a few more years to keep our linen shop where I helped her after school, my brother developed our father's contacts in the gold trade. He began to deal first with cultured pearls imported from Japan and later with diamonds from Antwerp, where a relative of ours was a trader in the local diamond exchange. David became a highly successful businessman who married the Israeli Vice-Consul to Rome in 1965; when their daughter Lea was due to start school in 1971, they moved to Tel Aviv where David joined the Diamond Bursa in Ramat Gan; he passed away in December 2019.

After graduating in chemical engineering from Rome University in 1964, thanks to the support of my brother, I was employed by a large multi-national oil company, ultimately as a company manager, until my retirement in 2002. After four years of being a councillor within the Rome Jewish Community and then the President of the Rome Jewish Hospital for one year, from the year 2000 until 2008 I was elected President of the Rome Jewish Community and from 2008 till 2015, President of the Foundation National Shoah Museum.

In 2016, my wife Giuliana and I made *aliyah*.
Leone Paserman, Jerusalem

My father Moszek Paserman

My mother Chana Cukier (1904-1976)

תעודת כבוד
Certificate of Honour

THIS IS TO CERTIFY THAT IN ITS SESSION OF OCTOBER 7, 2007 THE COMMISSION FOR THE DESIGNATION OF THE RIGHTEOUS, ESTABLISHED BY YAD VASHEM, THE HOLOCAUST HEROES & MARTYRS' REMEMBRANCE AUTHORITY, ON THE BASIS OF EVIDENCE PRESENTED BEFORE IT, HAS DECIDED TO HONOUR

Pietro Felici

WHO, DURING THE HOLOCAUST PERIOD IN EUROPE, RISKED HIS LIFE TO SAVE PERSECUTED JEWS.
THE COMMISSION, THEREFORE, HAS ACCORDED HIM THE MEDAL OF THE RIGHTEOUS AMONG THE NATIONS.
HIS NAME SHALL BE FOREVER ENGRAVED ON THE HONOUR WALL IN THE GARDEN OF THE RIGHTEOUS, AT YAD VASHEM, JERUSALEM.

Jerusalem, Israel
NOVEMBER 28, 2007

AVNER SHALEV
ON BEHALF OF THE YAD VASHEM DIRECTORATE

JACOB TURKEL
ON BEHALF OF THE COMMISSION FOR THE DESIGNATION OF THE RIGHTEOUS

Certificate of Honour

The cave where we hid for 7 months

Leone and Davide Paserman

Sami (Shalom) Prisant

His name was recorded on the Pentcho monument on the shores of Netanya as Shlomo and we were told that by that name our father boarded the Pentcho that sailed down the Danube and to the Aegean Sea.

But his real name is Shalom and his nick name—Sami.

At one point the ship began to sink but the captain of the ship managed to sail to a rocky island and all its passengers descended onto the island before the ship sank.

The passengers were stuck there for ten days; the women tied white sheets and with the help of boot polish were able to write the letters S.O.S. From the goodness of an Italian fighter who was flying overhead, the next day an Italian ship arrived and took them to the island of Rhodes where they stayed for over a year. From there they were taken to Ferramonti di Tarsia, in February 1942, where they were interred until the liberation of the camp by the allies in September 1943.

In 1944, our father managed to immigrate to Israel with the help of the Haganah Organization.

My mother Miriam (Mimi) Prisant (born Sternberg) was waiting for him and when he arrived in Israel they were married.

In 1945 my sister Yael was born and I, their daughter Edna, was born in 1951.

As a child I remember coming every year with my father for a meeting with the Pentcho group members at Café Tamar which was on Rothschild Boulevard, Tel Aviv.

May the memory of my father be blessed for ever.

Edna Blumenthal and Yael Sharon, Sami's daughters, Israel.

Prisant family

Sami and Mimi Prisant, Yael and Edna

Sultana Razon Veronesi

From the book "The heart, if it could think"
A story of love, research and battles
Translation of the excerpts by Simonetta Heger, with permission of the author.

Foreword

I must forget.

I must forget the years I spent in Italian and German concentration camps; I have to forget fear, hunger, physical and mental torture, that awful feeling of persecution that has continued to torment me since 1939; forget the long and disastrous illnesses of my family, of the sick children to whom I dedicated my life, and of the partner of my life.

I must also forget the difficulties and humiliations I met with, when I was trying to find work.

It has been a long and difficult fight.

I forget, but notwithstanding that, I write: and why? Everything has already been said about concentration camps, by qualified writers, in the fullest detail. But every single life is something different, unique.

I write to revive an extraordinary past, to make it come alive again, and to give a meaning to my existence, a life that maybe has been useful to some, or maybe totally useless.

I write for my children and my grandchildren, before the dust of forgetfulness and death comes to cover with their veil, the events, the thoughts and the experiences of a whole life.

My parents were married in Milan in 1931, and I was born in 1932, on a bright August day. My sister Vittoria was born three years later.

My parents and some of my maternal relatives had arrived in Milan from Istanbul at the beginning of the thirties; the first to arrive was Salomone, my mother's eldest brother, soon followed by my father. They had fled from Turkey just before being called up for military service, which consisted of five years of forced labour, in inhospitable areas. My mother arrived shortly after.

With Salomone's children I was bound, years later, to share the tragedies of war.

At seven, I had curls like Shirley Temple, but they were black instead of blonde, and my character was very rebellious and determined. In the morning I went to school in "Via Eupili" (the Milanese street where the Jewish school was situated) with tram number 1, and my mother and little sister accompanied me. In the afternoon we went walking.

One day in the autumn of 1939, I began to sense a nervousness in the family atmosphere: two big trunks suddenly made their appearance in the hallway, and Mother started filling them frantically. "Are we going away?" I kept asking.......finally, my father answered worriedly, "We are going to America, to visit your uncles". America was at that time a totally abstract concept for me.

The last months of 1939 were spent waiting, full of uncertainty and alarming news. In June 1940, Italy entered World War II as an ally of Germany against France and England. Germany was conquering territories, and applying racist persecution wherever the Nazis got into power. I knew nothing of that. I was only aware of bad moods and quarrels, and of my mother crying frequently. The trunks in the hall were always ready for departure, but they were never sent.

One evening, at the beginning of 1941, my father didn't come home. We waited in anguish throughout the night, and in the morning mother went to the Police: nothing. Then she searched all the hospitals, but to no avail. Days, weeks and months passed without news of him; my mother could not work, as schools were closed and my sister and I had nowhere else to go. Money began to get scarce, and then was gone completely. Finally, someone from the Jewish community told us that my father had been arrested in the street and, being a stateless Jew, had been sent to an internment camp in southern Italy, Ferramonti, about twenty miles from Cosenza in Calabria.

Decades later I would learn that Ferramonti di Tarsia was the largest Italian internment camp for foreign Jews built by the fascists, and the location had been chosen because of its remoteness from any military installation.

The camp was in the valley of the river Crati, in a swampy plain afflicted by malaria. Depending directly on the Ministry of Internal Affairs, it was ruled by a Commissioner, helped by a Marshall and a few policemen; the outer guard was entrusted to seventy-five soldiers of the fascist militia. The camp began operating on June 20th, 1940, ten days after Italy entered the war, and originally consisted of two barracks; the first internees, that had been taken prisoner in the large northern cities, found themselves in an isolated and unhealthy wasteland, far away from inhabited areas.

The barracks or camerata were built from a sort of wooden conglomerate called "carpilite" that had almost no power of insulation. A smaller concrete building contained the kitchen and the washroom; there were also a medical dispensary, a library, a courtroom and later a synagogue. Barbed wire ran along the entire perimeter of the camp, and there was also a watchtower. The railway line, connecting the inland with the Ionic coast and with Puglia, passed nearby.

My mother, my sister and I left our house and the trunks on the 24th of August, 1941, and boarded a train from Milan heading south; we were going to join my father. Our neighbours had helped us find the money for the journey. It was my ninth birthday, a warm day with a clear sky and glorious sunshine, and my sister and I were happy and excited by the novelty; only in later years we came to realize that the drastic decision of leaving without knowing or imagining the future, that my mother took suddenly, probably saved our lives. We were all three dressed as nicely as possible, and had taken with us only a small suitcase for what we considered only a brief summer trip. We had left the keys of our flat with the neighbours and the trunks with our belongings were still in the hall. We never saw them again....the house was wrecked by heavy bombing in August 1943.

We arrived at the gates of Ferramonti on a ramshackle carriage pulled by an old horse, the only means of transport we had found at the train station, after more than twenty-four hours of travelling and long stops in unknown places. Around the camp there was only open land, with a few sparse trees here and there.

I remember the guards' incredulous faces at my mother's request, to enter the camp followed by her two children; a rare case of voluntary incarceration. But what then looked like folly was in fact a very wise decision, dictated by love for her husband and the need to keep the family together. It most certainly saved the lives of us children.

Nobody could foresee the future or know the hell we were going to walk into, as did millions of other people, guilty only of not being born into the "pure" German Aryan race. The tight links that bound our family were fundamental in keeping us alive, encouraging and helping us to bear every sort of torture. My father's joy in seeing us arrive unexpectedly after months without any news from us, and our happiness in finding him, were indescribable. Mutual questions and answers overlapped in a whirlwind of excited voices, under the amused eyes of both guards and prisoners. Finally we embraced tightly, laughing convulsively.

The barracks, clean and white under the scorching sun, hosted a reasonable number of people and the bunks were comfortable enough. The camp busted with a frenzied activity: everybody was busy working or doing something useful for the community. The food was brought every morning from outside, on a cart pulled by a horse or, more often, by a donkey. Some of the internees were employed as cooks in the canteen, where they prepared meals for all the prisoners; others had reinvented themselves as shoemakers, tailors, farmers and nurses. The internees were allowed a large margin of self-management, provided it caused no disorder. It had been said that the relatively good life conditions were due to the good heart of the director and the goodwill of the marshall and guards. The local population was also very supportive of the internees; I remember a very active daily barter of foodstuffs such as oil, vegetables and fruit, exchanged for goods and handicrafts fashioned by the camp inmates.

My father, who had always traded in socks and stockings, started to breed turkeys, beginning with two specimens that quickly multiplied, and already numbered thirty by the time we arrived at the camp. My sister and I enjoyed watching them scratching around in the pen our father had constructed using a mixture of tree branches and wire.

The camp guards were very kind, and quite often allowed us, escorted by one of them, to ride on the cart up to the village to barter whatever was needed for the community of the inmates. I learned later that the director was finally removed from office because of his leniency towards the internees.

The first months in the camp were spent peacefully: new friendships were made, people studied, had discussions, improvised songs and dances at every festive occasion. Many old Jews met to study the Torah and Talmud, and some teachers organized lessons for children and youngsters to keep them active and their minds away from the uncertainty of our situation and loss of freedom. There was no money circulating; trade was based solely on bartering, and our turkeys proved very useful both as a source of food and a means of exchange.

As the time passed, the conditions of life in the camp began to deteriorate: water got scarce, and there were many cases of malaria; hunger was a daily drama as food diminished and the stock depleted.

We had spent our first year surrounded by barbed wire in a state of unconscious reality, a limbo that finished abruptly on a day in August 1942, as the order arrived for us to be transferred north to a small village in the province of Rovigo, named Taglio di Po.

In this little agricultural village our family was well accepted; we were assigned a small house and began a new life, poor but bearable, cultivating our own vegetables and raising chickens for their eggs. We two little girls went to school and made friends with local children.

A few months later the family was joined by our grandmother, our mother's older brother, Salomone, his wife Lea and their children Leone and Vittoria. They also had been taken by the police and sent to live in *confino libero*. We lived in Taglio di Po peacefully, albeit very poorly, for over a year, but with the armistice and the fascist social republic coming into power in northern Italy, things began to change: people became hostile, the school turned us away, and finally in November 1943 our parents were arrested by the fascists and taken to prison in Rovigo. I with my sister and cousins had to fend for ourselves, with no food and no-one to help us, and also nowhere to live as our house had been confiscated.

We were hosted at first by a local woman, then in a convent, but in February 1944 four fascists came for us and took us to the prison in Rovigo, where we were reunited with our family. Our joy was short-lived, as the day after we were taken to the concentration camp in Fossoli.

Drab, cold, muddy, it was very different from Ferramonti: people would arrive then suddenly depart, and in June our turn came to prepare for the same journey towards an unknown destination. We were told to be ready to leave at six in the morning. For the first time I saw the infamous Nazis, and for the first time I was really scared, by their malevolent glances, their shouts, their unprovoked violence.

We were forced to climb into cattle wagons, and our terrible journey began; we knew we were heading north. While still in Italy people seeing the train would sometimes call out a kind word to us, but as soon as we heard German spoken during our stops, no-one had a shred of pity anymore. The first words that I heard stepping down from that wagon were, "schnell, schnell, raus!"

In 1980 I happened to be in Vienna to see an opera, and at the end the ushers urged us to leave the theatre saying those same words: I nearly fainted from the anguish.

The scene was illuminated by enormous headlights, but beyond them it was total darkness; no moon, no stars, only shouts, curses and desperate cries filled the air. We were entering the camp of Bergen-Belsen.

We walked in twos in a long trail of people, paralyzed by fear; nevertheless my father carefully observed the proceedings and with his intuition he saved all our lives. He made a sign to us to show to the Nazis, not our documents saying that we were stateless, but our old Turkish passports, that we had guarded during all those years even if they had expired. In 1944 Turkey was neutral and collaborating with Germany; the SS were perplexed. They wanted to divide the family and send grandmother and us children to the gas chambers, but unsure, they put us all in a fenced-off part of the camp. There the prisoners coming from neutral countries such as Turkey, Switzerland, Spain and Greece were kept, in no better conditions than the others, but at least they were left alive and families were not separated.

We managed to survive through the cruelty, the cold, the tortures, the illnesses, the hunger and all the worst things that a human being can endure, thanks only to our being together. Our parents kept our minds busy, to try to avert them from the horror we were living. They exchanged their meagre rations of soup with another prisoner who gave French lessons to me and my sister; these lessons were precious, a semblance of real life for young people who observed every sort of aberration with innocent eyes, unable to remember that there could be a life different from the present nightmare. I think that during those years I must have stopped growing both physically and mentally; it's the only way I can explain the impression I had that the only existing reality was the one we were living, that the word "freedom" had no sense whatsoever, and that nowhere in the world could one live without hunger or despair.

In March 1945 the situation was getting worse every day; typhoid fever, dysentery, tuberculosis and pneumonia raged over exhausted and broken bodies. I wanted to help the sick, but could not, and it was at that point I decided that I wanted to become a doctor. But I too got ill, contracting tuberculosis as I approached my thirteenth birthday. We started hearing the bombing getting nearer, the SS became more cruel and none of the new arrivals were left alive, they all were sent immediately to the gas chambers.

I don't think many witnesses remain who can speak of Bergen-Belsen, unlike Auschwitz or Mauthausen, because it was the worst lager of all, and there were almost no survivors.

At the beginning of May, 1945, we were summoned for appeal, and an unknown SS officer read a list of names on a sheet of paper he extracted from a brown leather bag; many of the names did not have an owner anymore, but we were among those still alive. We didn't know what we had been called for. Mass shooting? Gas chamber selection? To be transported to another lager? At the end we were taken to the showers, trembling and convinced that it was the end, but to our surprise and joy it was water, not gas, that came out of the shower heads.

We were given civilian clothing, obviously taken from gas chamber victims; then we were put onto buses and driven to the station. There a train was waiting for us. During the long hours on the train the SS gave us some food, thinking that they could so quickly amend years of malnutrition. My mother cleverly advised us to eat little, and not all at once, to let our stomachs adapt to solid food, and we obeyed; some people who ate too fast got ill almost instantly and died.

We finally arrived in Sweden, and were told that we were part of an exchange between prisoners interned in Germany and German residents in Turkey, as this country had recently entered war against Germany.

The Swedish people who welcomed us could not believe what the survivors told them; they couldn't imagine such depths of cruelty. I cannot remember our stay in Sweden, as I was very ill, but I know that as I got better and all of us were beginning to get stronger we embarked on a ship called Stockholm headed to Istanbul. It was the beginning of our coming back to life.

Sultana Razon Veronesi
First published in Milan, Italy – BUR 2014 RCS Libri

Sultana Veronesi

David Ropschitz

David Henryk Ropschitz (1913-1986)

My father, David Ropschitz, was born in Lwow, Galicia, in 1913, the youngest of Moses (born 1865) and Sofia Ropschitz's (born Juweles, 1871) 10 children. Galicia at the time was part of the Austro-Hungarian Empire and Lwow was a thriving cultural and commercial centre with a Jewish population of over 100,000.

My great-grandfather David Hirsch Ropschitz was an orthodox tailor who loved to spend his time in Talmudic study, but his son Moses was more interested in providing for his large family than studying Torah. He was a goldsmith who over time, owned several properties in Lwow and ran his own jewellery business in the city's Jewish quarter before moving his family to Vienna when my father was only a few years old.

The following information I have put together through several years of family history research. My father rarely spoke about his early life and most children seem oblivious to their parents' past, only regretting their lack of interest when it's too late to find answers.

This is a brief resumé of his 9 siblings born between 1891 and 1913. His oldest sister Amalia (Malka) born 1891 married Ludwig Merkel, a lawyer. They had three children, Stefaniya, Josif and Runa.

Sister Klara (Tushka) born 1892 married a man by the name of Todt.

Brother Eduard born 1894 served and was decorated in the First World War.

Brother Isydor born 1895 studied medicine at the University of Padua, Italy. He married Rosa Breitman and moved to Alassio, on the Italian Riviera, in 1926 where he built a thriving medical practice. In 1938 to escape Nazi persecution, the family moved to Brisbane, Australia where they changed their name to the less conspicuously Jewish name of Roxon.

Sister Roza, born 1897, married Samuel Rauch and I think they had 3 children, Hermann, Ignacy and Henrjetta.

Brother Leon, born 1898, completed medical studies in Italy like his brothers, moved with wife Pepi and daughter Rita (born 1929) to USA to escape Nazi persecution in Italy and worked as a doctor in New York until his death.

Brother Mundek born 1901, worked in the family jewellery business in Vienna but took his own life in 1930.

Sister Helena, born in 1903, married a Jewish doctor and moved to Bordighera on the Italian Riviera then escaped Nazi persecution in South Africa, returning many years later to live out her life in Brussels.

Sister Anna, born in 1907, also married a Jewish doctor, Frederick Nussenblatt, and moved to Viareggio. She spent the war years in hiding while her son Enrico was brought up by monks in a local monastery. After the war the family was reunited in Genoa and another son, Emanuele, was born.

Finally my father, born in 1913 in Lwow, moved to Vienna as a young boy. He attended the Zwi Perez Chajes Realgymnasium and later followed 4 of his older siblings to Italy where he studied medicine at the University of Genoa completing his studies just before the racial laws of 1938 were passed, preventing him obtaining work as a doctor.

In 1940 he was arrested and sent to Ferramonti di Tarsia where he was to spend the next 3 years.

His time in Ferramonti has been chronicled in his autobiographical novel, *Ferramonti: Salvation behind the barbed wire*, written in his last years and published in 2020. As my father changed all the names of the characters, it has been a challenge to identify them; I am constantly searching.

My father was among the first to arrive in Ferramonti in July 1940 when it was still under construction with no proper water supply and open latrines. He was appointed the Capo of his camerata which I believe was number 3. Over time, Ferramonti became the multi-cultural community described by so many. Despite the Spartan living conditions, the malaria, the gnawing hunger, the heat in summer and cold in winter and the constant anxiety of war and fear for family left behind, the internees led a relatively autonomous life.

In October 1941 my father was among a group of internees sent to *confino libero* in Notaresco which was like paradise in comparison. He relished the cooler Abruzzi air, more plentiful food, freedom to walk around the little town, drink proper coffee and read the paper in the local café, and chat to the locals. Even better, upon his arrival he was reunited with an old school chum from Vienna, Albert Goldfield, who had been in Notaresco for the past year. There was no barbed wire; my father even had his own room with a balcony as the only fully qualified doctor among the internees. Life was almost normal. But then in May 1942 it all came to an abrupt end and he found himself back in Ferramonti, again with no explanation, although in his book he attributes this sudden punishment to the absconding of one individual from the group.

By the time my father had returned to Ferramonti, the Pentcho ship with its cargo of over 400 had already arrived and the camp was unrecognisable, the cultural mix had changed and Polish was no longer the dominant language. The food rations had become further depleted and people were now very hungry indeed. A few people still had money to buy from the camp stores or to barter but my father had long since run out of funds. He had spent 2 years in hiding after the Racial Laws of 1938 so had no money to fall back on.

However, he applied and was accepted to join a working party collecting firewood in fields some distance away from the camp. This not only got him out of the close confines of the camerata which he shared with another 30 males with its stifling heat and the interminable aggravation of flies and mosquitoes, but more importantly earned him a few lire and introduced him to the black market currency which was rife. During the work breaks, far away from the camp itself, the wood collecting internees bartered their worldly goods under the eyes of the militia who took their own cut of the transactions. They would return in the evening, after a day's labours under the hot Calabrian sun, with a few eggs, some olive oil, a chunk of bread, some flour, some sausage. Unfortunately the trips out to the woods came to an end after another escape attempt by an internee.

In July 1943 after the 'friendly fire' incident which caused 4 fatalities and many more injured, many internees, in fear for their lives, ran to the neighbouring hills and villages where the local people took them in most generously, sharing their food and lives with them. My father and a couple he had grown close to, (a diabetic man from Zagreb and his much younger German-speaking wife of whom I have many photos but no names — see photo below) ran away to the hills where they spent the next few weeks living with a widow of Albanian descent and her young daughter in a tiny stone house. My father described this hideaway amid verdant pastures, abundant fig trees, a stream and nearby grotto as a bucolic idyll.

In time my father would make calls to visit the sick in neighbouring villages with the widow, despite his protestations, leading him on her donkey.

Once the camp of Ferramonti was liberated in September 1943, internees began to return from their hilltop hideouts. Apart from the regular supply of cigarettes and chocolate, the British had doubled the food rations for the internees while sadly halving them for the local Italian population, now the vanquished enemy, despite them having been, on the whole, kind and hospitable to the Ferramonti prisoners.

Much has been written about the humane treatment the internees received at the hands of the Italians in comparison with Nazi brutality. Even though the residents of Ferramonti were not subjected to forced labour or cruelty, Ferramonti was no holiday camp or kibbutz. Its fluctuating population, reckoned around 2,000 at the time of liberation, were prisoners behind barbed wire, and permanently hungry. That they had football tournaments despite their malnourishment, created synagogues and schools for the many children, gave concerts, exhibitions, plays, opened rudimentary cafes and laundries, is a testament to their talent, industrious spirit of enterprise, and dogged determination to survive.

After the liberation, many internees left the camp as soon as they could. Some could not wait to return to defend their homeland against the Nazis. This seemed to be particularly the case with the Yugoslav contingent. According to the paperwork from the liberating 8th Army archives, the majority of males wanted to return to Yugoslavia. Others went north in search of their lost families, often with tragic consequences as the Germans were now stationed in Milan and would deport any Jews to their deaths. Those who remained in Ferramonti in the hope of getting to Palestine or other places were safe. In 1944 almost a thousand Jewish refugees boarded the US Henry Gibbons in Naples bound for Fort Ontario, Oswego, New York despite the risks from German U boat patrols.

Ferrramonti camp remained open under allied protection until December 1945.

After Ferramonti was liberated, my father returned to helping the sick in the local communities in the hilltop villages staying with his kindly Albanian hostess who I have been unable to identify. When he finally took his leave, he joined the British army in Taranto in 1944 as an interpreter and then eventually in Treviso was promoted to Captain in the Royal Army Medical Corps, North Africa division.

I don't know at what point he found out, but my father's elderly parents, his 3 older sisters Amalia, Klara and Rosa, and his brother Edi, and their spouses and children, had all been murdered presumably in Auschwitz. After the Anschluss, they had left Vienna and returned to their previous home in Lwow where they still had some properties and probably felt safer than in Vienna. In the end, Lwow was decimated and out of the population of roughly 150,000 Jews in 1940 less than 1,000 remained after the war. This fate was repeated all over Europe. The collective trauma of entire families being so cruelly wiped out is unimaginable.

The only one from that branch of the Ropschitz family to have survived was my cousin Stefania, (Stenya) the oldest daughter of Amalia and Ludwig Merkel who aged about 18 jumped off the cattle wagon which was taking her parents and younger sister to their deaths.

Her brother Jusif Merkel had been a practising physician before the Nazi occupation. In despair after losing his parents and younger sister, he took poison. Stefania changed her name to Jusifa after the war to honour his memory. She married a Russian soldier, Arkady Karastishefski and they had two children who moved from Lwow where they had grown up to Israel after the death of their father. With the help of Avner Halevy whose contribution can also be found in this book, in 2020 I discovered Jusifa's son Anatoly and daughter Miriam were living in Ashdod; I look forward to meeting them one day very soon. It will be an emotional occasion to connect with the last remnants of the Ropschitz family of Lwow.

After being demobbed my father came to London where he met my mother Violet, a glamorous fashion model; they married in 1949 and had three children, my 2 brothers and me.

Initially working as a GP in London, he then moved into psychiatry thanks to time spent with Dr Ernst Bernhard in Ferramonti who taught him psychoanalytic techniques. Over the years his work in this field took him north, to Liverpool, Derby, Huddersfield and Halifax as a consultant psychiatrist, with a particular interest in suicide, perhaps as a result of the loss of his brother Mundek in 1930. His work on the Gold Watch Syndrome, which focused on the higher suicide rate in males after retirement, was published in 1968.

My father was a difficult man to live with, perhaps not surprisingly. Being the youngest child of 10 in a middle class, East European family, he was probably spoilt, and had absorbed some of the attitudes to women prevalent in those times. The holistic education he had received in Vienna made him value learning above all else, scolding me and my brothers if we displayed ignorance. He was a lover of classical music, opera, literature, art and travel. He knew his classics, history of ancient civilisations and world geography. Every Friday night at the Sabbath table we had "Questions" during which our father quizzed us in General Knowledge. My brothers and I loved it although as my father pointed out, we only liked it when we got the answers right. At bedtime, he read us stories of Greek mythology so we fell asleep with tales of Medusa, the Minotaur and other monsters ringing in our ears. The tragic tale of Niobe and her slain 14 children who was eventually turned to stone for her pride, was one that I never forgot, no matter how hard I tried!

My father reconnected with his old friend Albert Goldfield in the 1980s. They planned a trip to Ferramonti for 1986 but my father had developed cancer and died in September 1986 at the age of 73, leaving his "Ferramonti" manuscript unpublished. I

am sure he would have been delighted to know it finally saw the light of day.
Yolanda Ropschitz-Bentham, Somerset, England

My father, his sister Helena and their nephew Jusif on the Bordighera promenade before the war

Three doctors in Ferramonti. Ropschitz, Klein and Friedmann

With mystery woman in Ferramonti

Captain D H Ropschitz, 1945, RAMC

July 1986, 2 months before his death from cancer

Amalia and Aron Schöps

Ruth Rosenzweig writes....

I was born in Vienna on May 4, 1933. Towards the end of 1936, my parents, Amalia and Aron Schöps, sold their two bedding stores and moved the family to Milano, Italy. In Italy, my father made a living importing down. We had a very nice apartment at Via Teodosio, 60.

Italy went to war in 1940. The racial laws had come out in 1938, but they weren't really enforced until they entered the war, and even then only partially.

In first grade, my father used to walk me to school at Via Della Spiga, which was a building that, I believe, the Jewish community either rented or bought because we were not allowed to go to public school. In February 1940, my brother was born. I named him Umberto because we had a royal prince named Umberto who I adored. (My mom told the nurse that her mother wanted to name the baby Umberto, so they put that name on the birth certificate—Joy).

In the summer of 1940, my father was arrested. My mother found out that he was being sent to an internment camp in southern Italy, Ferramonti in Tarsia. She believed that Italians would not harm women and children, so her husband would be safer if the family was with him. She went to the police department and said that she wanted to join her husband. They said, "Go ahead and join him." I remember the train trip south with my mother and baby brother.

We arrived in Ferramonti. Every family was assigned a barrack. I remember there was something like a white sheet separating the area where we slept from the area where my mother cooked. She cooked on charcoal. We slept on boards or doors resting on bricks and covered with straw. The barracks were whitewashed. I remember sticking my fingers in the wall and seeing what looked like tiny shredded paper or straw inside.

Every morning we were given a small pill that looked like a light blue M&M - quinine. I found out years later that there were swamps in Ferramonti and these pills prevented us from contracting malaria. We would also get 8 lire per adult and 4 lire per child every day. I assume my mother bought food and some other necessities with it.

The camp was surrounded by what looked like 2 chicken wires—one below my knees and one a little above my head. We children used to climb through and go play in the fields-pick flowers and things like that. The Marshall who ran the camp used to come with open trucks and take us for a few hours in the afternoon to nearby fields, so we kids could run around and play.

A teacher in the camp taught me the Hebrew prayers for thunder and lightning, which I still recite today.

My family remained in Ferramonti for about a year and then was moved to Camisano Vicentino, which is close to Vicenza. Supposedly, we were not allowed to leave that town without permission. But I don't remember having a permission slip or any other form with me when I took the school bus to Vicenza, the closest big city.

In Camisano, they put us and three other families in one huge, beautiful villa. There were the Steins, with two daughters, the Holzers, with a son and a daughter, and Fleisig, with a daughter. My grandmother was with us in Camisano, but I don't know when she joined us because I don't remember her in Ferramonti.

Mom became pregnant again in 1942. Because Umberto was a Caesarean, there was a risk her delivery might be a bit difficult. So somebody wrote to Mussolini asking for permission to let her give birth in a hospital. Permission was granted and my sister, Diana, was born in Padova.

In Camisano, my father raised geese. One other family tried ducks, but there was a small river along the big garden, so they swam away. Another couple tried raising chicks, but they got sick and all died. Pop's geese did very well. I also remember a beautiful garden with apple and pear trees.

One of my aunts sent me a bicycle with my cousin Herbie when he came to visit. He came again a couple of times and I went to visit his family. Eventually, my uncle Ziggy went back to Milano, because he was sick or something, and my grandmother got permission to go and visit him.

After school, I used to play with many children in the town. (She returned many years later with my dad and had a wonderful reunion with some of them- Joy) After the war, I learned that following the armistice in September '43, the mayor of Camisano spoke to the Jews in town and told them to get ready to leave. He said that they should pack only what they could carry and travel south. The Germans were heading in their direction and the Jews needed to get to the Allies in the south before the Nazis arrived. The mayor said he would send somebody to let them know when to depart. And that's what happened. I remember one night we got dressed, left, and travelled south by bus and by train. At one point, the rails had been bombed and destroyed so we travelled via a horse drawn cart. We would go to small towns, find the local priests, and tell them we were Jews running away from the Germans. The priests would find us places to stay.

We ended up in Folignano, which is near Ascoli Piceno. The priest knew of a house up on a hill that wasn't being used. We hid out in that house until the end of the war. My mother gave birth, but there was no doctor available, just an inexperienced medical student, and he accidentally killed the baby when removing him with forceps.

Joy Rosenzweig writes....

At the end of the war, my mom and her family came down from the house on the hill in a horse drawn cart. Unfortunately, the people who swept that hill for landmines missed one, and the cart went over it. My aunt Diana fell out of my mom's arms and her head went under the wheel of the cart. My mom pulled her out, but wrecked her leg in the process. She ended up in bed for about 8 months, but miraculously, didn't need to have it amputated.

After the war, my grandmother ran a home for Jewish orphans called Sciesopoli, in Selvino. She made sure the kids had medical and psychological services, clean clothing, and Jewish comfort food. They were then sent to Israel[*].

---

[*] cf. www.en.wikipedia.org/wiki/Selvino_children

Afterwards, the family returned to Milano. My grandmother started a company making foundation undergarments and bathing suits.

My mother came to New York in 1953, when she was 19, because she had wanted to attend university here. She found a job working for my father's brother who had started a ribbon trimmings business. My uncle introduced my parents to each other and they were married within the year. I was born in 1959 and my brother in 1960.

My dad, Gary Rosenzweig, had immigrated to the United States from Czernowitz (now Chernivtsi, Ukraine), a few years before my mom arrived. After my parents were married, he enlisted in the army and was stationed at Fort Hamilton, NY. Following his service, he joined the family business and worked alongside my mother until she left to raise my brother and me. My parents worked together again in 1963-4, when we moved to Brescia to build up the Italian branch of the business.

Other than during those 9 months in Brescia, my mother was a homemaker and stay-at-home mom. She didn't become an engineer as she had planned, but put her construction and creative talents to use building wooden cabinets for our toys, a vanity for me, extensions for tables, and a chuppah (with the aid of another congregant) for the first wedding at the synagogue that my parents helped found. She sewed dresses for me in styles and colours that inevitably became popular one or two years later. Everyone in the family has one of her embroidered tablecloths.

My father passed away in 1999. My mom currently lives in Queens, NY. She enjoys reading, history, foreign languages, going to Manhattan, and spending time with her kids and grandkids.

Ruth and Joy Rosenzweig, USA

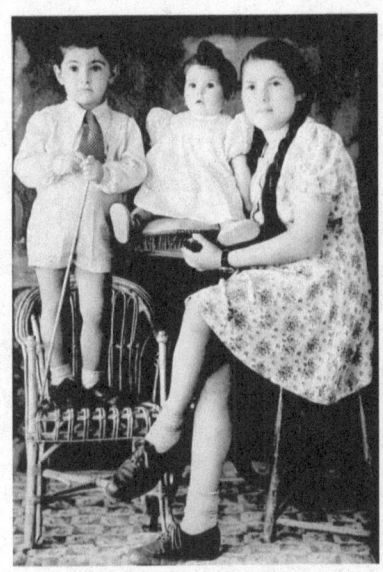

Ruth age 10 with siblings Umberto and Diana, Camisano, 1943

Diana, Ruth and Umberto

Ruth and Gary 1953

...and 1994

Mordechai Schwartz

Here is the story of my grandfather, Emerich (Mordechai) Schwartz. He was born on the 26th of June, 1922, in Czechoslovakia, today's Slovakian state, in the town of Košice.

Born as Emerich, his middle name was Mordechai, after his great grandfather, later adopted as his first name. He had two brothers, but his older brother died in 1928 when Mordechai was just seven. In 1933, during the great depression, which seriously affected their lives, the family moved to Bratislava, where they opened a store. However, a year and a half later, when he was 12, his parents divorced. This meant that since his father was a Hungarian citizen, he had to leave Czechoslovakia and move to Budapest. His mother, Gizela, stayed in Bratislava with him and his younger brother, creating a "broken family" in the words of my grandfather. The relationship between his parents was dreadful; this had a profound effect on his childhood.

Seeing his mother struggling with the small family subsistence, Mordechai left school at 13 to learn a profession. His mother wanted him to become an engraver, a family tradition. However, since he was very good with his hands, he told his mother that he would rather be a mechanic. In the end his mother contacted his father in Hungary, and they decided Mordechai should go to Hungary to learn a proper trade. In 1936, his mother handed him over to his father on the Czechoslovakian-Hungarian border. It was the last time his parents ever met.

At first Mordechai lived at his aunt's house, working in a grocery and hardware store. In the meantime, he was looking to learn a decent trade. He mainly wanted to be a jeweller, a goldsmith. In Budapest in those days, there was an "open" newspaper on the main street that those who could not afford to buy could read for free. One day, he stopped to look and found an advertisement for a jeweller's apprentice. The jeweller, a bachelor called Emerich (same as he was) Ast, was a talented professional, a designer, a setter, and an engraver – all were connected in the jewellery business, and Mordechai was happy to learn from him.

When Ast asked him after a few weeks what he would like to be, Mordechai replied he wanted to be a jeweller. So Ast sent him for some professional aptitude testing. During an eight hour assessment he was tested in mathematics and craft skills, such as bending wires and fine art. At the end of that day, there were two options: you either received a pink slip, which meant you failed, or a yellow slip, which meant you passed. Mordechai got the yellow and so he started his apprenticeship.

For the first five weeks, all he did was scrub the floor and buy his boss cigarettes. Mordechai described Mr Ast as pleasant but with a sadistic streak. Ast used to hit him occasionally, especially if he thought he was not concentrating enough when leaning on the bench. "Emerich! Watch me!" he would yell at him. Eventually, he asked Mordechai to call his father.

Mordechai's father was a salesman for a big company and used to travel all over Hungary. In mid-February 1936, he met Ast and signed a contract with him to start the apprenticeship officially. According to the agreement, Mordechai was to be paid a monthly salary of 6 Pengő in the first year, 9 in the second year, and 13 Pengő in the third year. The Pengő was the official Hungarian currency between 1927 to 1946 until the Forint replaced it. During that time, it was enough to buy himself a daily bowl of hot beetroot soup.

After his aunt told his father that she couldn't afford to keep him anymore, Mordechai moved to an out-of-town hostel for young people who had come from all over Hungary to learn a trade in the capital. He slept on the bottom of two bunk-beds and although the hostel conditions were not that bad, the guy on the top bunk hated him and would urinate on him from above, calling him a "stinking Jew."

At the hostel, they were given breakfast and a ticket for lunch or dinner in the city. Their diet in those days was mainly based around horse meat. The daily life at the hostel was very strict. There was a curfew after 21:00, and those who were late could find themselves spending the night on the street. Mordechai spent about two and half years there. In 1939, he finished his apprenticeship and went back to his mother in Bratislava with his diploma in his hand.

His mother had no room for him to stay with her as she slept on a bed at the back of her store, using the toilets outside, so she rented a room for him with a family in the city, and he started working at a jewellery store. He worked there for nine months throughout 1939, mostly making foundations for gold designs. He earned a good salary which he gave to his mother, who paid for his room, food and all he needed. At lunchtime, the store was closed for two hours; he collected food from a restaurant nearby, soup and a main course, which he and his mother ate together.

One day, the store was full of customers when a gentleman walked in. His name was Zoltan Schalk. He said, "Mrs Schwartz, do you have a son here? I heard that he is a jeweller. Would you like to send him to Palestine?" Schalk talked to his mother for a while, and she promised to speak to her son.

"Emerich," she told him, "you know what is going on here with the anti-Semitism." It was the end of 1939, and the situation was deteriorating rapidly, and they were afraid to walk outside in the evenings. Mordechai had never been a member of any of the Jewish organisations, such as Hashomer Hatzair or Beitar. He never thought of leaving Czechoslavakia, then already the Slovak state, as Nazi Germany seized the Czech part. At his mother's request, he went to look at the place Schalk had told her about but did not go inside. One of his mother's customers, a lovely lady, was the wife of the head of the Bratislava police department. They were friends, and his mother told her about Schalk's offer to send Mordechai to Palestine. One day, a policeman on a bicycle came by the store. He handed a letter to Mordechai's mother from the director of the police department. It was a Saturday, and by coincidence, Mordechai himself was in the store. It was an invitation for him and his mother to come to the office of Jacob Botzi, the head of the police department. Mordechai put on his best clothes and went with his mother to the meeting. His mother went inside and talked to the commander while he waited on the bench outside. After a while, she came out and asked him to go into the commander's room. Inside, Mr Botzi was very nice to him, and after a few minutes, he asked him directly, "Would you like to go to Palestine?"

Mordechai did not want to go. However, since he saw the situation around him and his mother's wish, he said yes. Mr Botzi picked up the telephone, called someplace and said in Slovak that he is looking to issue a passport for someone. Then, he called the NZO, the New Zionist Organisation, and asked to speak to someone. He said that they had to take Mordechai on the ship or it would not be allowed to set sail from Bratislava. He told Mordechai to come back on Wednesday in his best clothes and gave him an exit permit. It was a one-way visa out of Slovakia, with no return.

After some delays, the ship, "Pentcho," set sail from the port of Bratislava on the 18th of May, 1940. The tales of the Pentcho are well documented in Yehoshua Halevi's book "Habayta". Suffice it to say that after many adventures along the Danube, the Black Sea and the Aegean Sea, almost two years after departing from Bratislava, the passengers arrived in camp Ferramonti di Tarsia in Calabria, Italy, in early March 1942.

In Ferramonti, they had a quiet camp life, nothing like the Polish and German concentration camps. Mordechai, who had a talent for languages, was soon speaking Italian. He adapted to daily life in the camp, playing football with his friend Bernard (Booby) Feder.

After the liberation of the camp in September 1943, Mordechai and Booby were occasionally allowed to travel to Bari, trading cigarettes, figs and dates with the locals and inside the camp. At nights, he would lie on his bunk in the crowded barrack, a bag full of figs as his pillow, eating them until his stomach ached. In time, he accepted the offer to join the Czech division of the British army, thinking it would bring him closer to returning to Czechoslovakia and back to his mother. Little did he know she had already perished in Auschwitz.

He sailed to the UK for initial training as a soldier in autumn 1943. He became a "loader" in M4 Sherman tanks, and shortly after, he was sent to Normandy, France, on D-day. In August 1944, he was back in the UK for additional military training. Travelling on the tube to the base, he suddenly felt very ill. He was diagnosed with malaria, apparently caught at Ferramonti, and sent to a London military hospital. With a red cross on her hat, a beautiful nurse took care of him for a whole month, but he was too weak to talk to her. When his friend Booby visited him, Mordechai pointed to her and said that it is too bad she was not Jewish. Booby told him that not only was she Jewish, but she was a refugee from Czechoslovakia. Her name was Esther, and on the 11th of November, they were married in London. Four days later, he was back in France as part of the occupying force.

On the 15th of July 1945, their son Zvi was born. They lived in the UK for two months after the war and moved to Belgium, where Esther had some family who had managed to survive. In 1947 their daughter, Pnina, was born, and in 1949, the family immigrated to the young state of Israel. The first year was rough; the young family lived first in a tent, in a camp near Herzliya, and later in a wooden hut. It was hot in the summer, cold and muddy in the winter, and toilets were shared with the neighbours. Emerich, who had now changed his name to Mordechai, could not find a job as a jeweller. For a few years, he worked in road construction, as a night guard, at a blacksmith's workshop, and later at a factory for silverware tools. Only in 1956 did he finally find a job as a jeweller in Petah Tikvah.

In 1958 they moved to a tiny house in Ramleh. Mordechai began working for a jeweller on 81 Allenby Street, in Tel Aviv. Working from his desk at home, he occasionally travelled to the workshop in Allenby Street to collect orders and the strips of gold. Sometimes, he sent his son, Zvi, to bring the gold to him. He thrived at work, and his artistic nature was reflected in his creations. Apart from the rings, necklaces and other "regular" jewellery, he made miniatures of musical instruments. Those were once presented in an exhibition in Tel Aviv that even Ben Gurion came to see.

But with the recession in Israel in the early 60s he lost his job. Daughter Pnina, moved to the US in 1965 and shortly after, in 1966, Mordechai got a job offer in Manhattan, on 47th Street. In April 1967, he travelled to the US with Esther. Zvi, who was in his military service, was supposed to follow them on his release but met his future wife and stayed in Israel.

Mordechai and Esther lived in Rego Park, Queens; he travelled daily to his work to Manhattan. During the 70s, he became progressively weaker due to heart disease. In 1978, he had a major coronary artery bypass, which improved his condition dramatically. He continued to work on 47th Street until his retirement in 1992. He and Esther then moved to New Jersey to live near Pnina. He died in 2010 at the age of 88, eighteen months after his wife.

Esther and Mordechai are survived by their children, Zvi and Pnina, and grandchildren Eitan, Erez and Nurit (of Zvi), Lisa and Ronnie (of Pnina). Ronnie had the opportunity to film Mordechai on his last day, speaking of his childhood. Many details here are taken from that film.

Eitan Segev, Jerusalem

Pre-war, Gizela Schwartz outside Bratislava shop

Imre and Gizela with sons Baruch (left) and Emerich

Booby (left) at Esther and Mordechai's wedding in 1944

Zvi and Mina's wedding, Esther and Mordechi right, Pnina with husband and baby, left.

Mordechai and his father, Hungary, 1973

Esther and Mordechai, 2007

Yehuda Spiegel

Yehuda Spiegel was born Leopold Spiegel on July 29th, 1929, in Bratislava, Slovakia. His first-born sister was Rosalia, and after her five younger brothers were born, of whom he was the youngest.

His father was a wine merchant. His oldest brother, Isaac, joined the Republican fighters in the Spanish Civil War, and after their defeat he left and joined the Czech division of the Red Army, fighting against Germany. He was killed in Kiev when he ordered his battalion to retreat from the advancing German tanks, located himself in the middle of a street and fired on the tanks until they ran over and killed him. His battalion managed to escape and survived.

The second brother, Moshe, immigrated to Palestine in the 1930s, worked in agriculture, joined the Hebrew Battalion of the British army and fought against Germany with them.

The other three brothers remained with their parents but their sister, who was working in the Slovakian Betar headquarters and helping to organise the Pentcho sailing, took two of her brothers with her on the trip to Palestine. Yehuda's second-youngest brother, Joseph, remained with his parents who refused to abandon their home, hoping that the situation would improve. It did not. Joseph was sent to Theresienstadt concentration camp and murdered there, and his parents were sent to Auschwitz where they too were murdered. The two brothers Eliezer (Onki) and Yehuda joined their sister, who by then had taken the Hebrew name Shoshana, and sailed on the Pentcho with her. Yehuda was not yet 11 when they sailed off from Bratislava in May 1940. Four months later the Pentcho had a power accident, hit a rocky island in the Aegean sea and sank. The passengers, who all managed to get safely onto the island, were saved later by the Italians who shipped them to Rhodes.

In January 1942 the Italians transported them to Italy. Yehuda was 12 years old and he was among the first group of

200 women, children, the old and the sick, who boarded the ship Kalimno on its journey to Ferramonti.

As a child in Ferramonti, Yehuda went to the school that detainees founded there, liked to learn mathematics, and had lessons playing the piano too. He took part in the Betar youth movement and participated in their activities, learning the history and geography of Israel and the Hebrew language too. Yehuda was a keen sportsman who played in the youth football team as a goalkeeper. He was a strong swimmer too; he would sometimes leave the camp to swim in the Crati river which flowed nearby. The Italian camp commanders permitted the detainees — under some surveillance — to cool down from the intense Calabrian heat with a dip in the river.

When he reached Palestine in May 1944, his sister Shoshana could not raise him on her own in the tiny wash room where she lived with her husband Yehoshua. She found a Kibbutz, Maaleh Hachamisha, near Jerusalem, where Yehuda, aged 15, lived and joined their youth group. He was active in Kibbutz life and in its defence against hostile people around it. Together with a few friends they took upon themselves the challenge of walking a few miles westwards where they founded a new Kibbutz, Neveh Ilan.

The State of Israel was established exactly four years after his arrival there, and when the War of Independence broke out he joined the army, where he continued to serve after the war too. His work involved training and qualifying young boys and girls to serve in the armed forces, and combined his service with his hobby — walking long distances and touring large areas around the new State of Israel. In the army he met Yaffa from Jerusalem whom he later married.

After his army duties Yehuda studied education and teaching, later becoming a teacher himself. He was sent overseas several times, twice to South America and then to Europe, to help Jewish communities learn Hebrew, Jewish history and the geography of the State of Israel.

Yehuda and Yaffa settled in Nathanya, Israel. He was promoted several times by the Ministry of Education and was Head Principal of several schools until his retirement.

Yehuda and Yaffa have four children and eight grandchildren. They now live in Modiin, close to their two younger daughters and their families.
Avner Halevy, Israel

Young Yehuda in Ferramonti: Betar group and Talmud Torah

Yehuda in Kibbutz Neveh Ilan

Yehuda and Yaffa with granddaughter

Shlomo and Sara Zelmanovitch

During World War II, when the Germans occupied more and more countries in Europe, 500 young Jewish people from Bratislava, Czechoslovakia, decided to make *aliyah* to Eretz-Israel. All of them were members of *Betar*. Among them were my parents, Sarah Bonitzer, age 18 and Shlomo Zelmanovitch, 23 years old.

They left in May 1940 and sailed for six months on the Danube steamer ship Pentcho, reaching first the Black Sea then the Aegean Sea, where it ran aground on the uninhabited rocky island of Camilo Nisi. Luckily all the passengers survived. After 9 days they were rescued by an Italian ship and transported to the island of Rhodes.

Sarah and Shlomo were married in Rhodes and after a year under very bad conditions, the Pentcho travellers were sent from Rhodes to Ferramonti di Tarsia camp, in southern Italy.

The Nazis made many attempts to have the Jews from Ferramonti dispatched to the extermination camps, but when the Italians saw the fate of Jews in the north, they refused to cooperate. So the people were saved and they remained in Ferramonti until the end of the war. I, their daughter Eva, was born on 11th April 1944, in Ferramonti di Tarsia camp.

The internees of Ferramonti were treated humanely. They received food, medicine and whatever could make their situation easier, while the Italian people also had very little to survive on during the war.

My parents Shlomo and Sarah Zelmanovitch, left Italy for Palestine in May 1945, from Bari, on the ship "Princess Katherine." They arrived with me, a 13 month old baby, in Atlit, near Haifa, where there was a camp for the displaced European Jews who came to Israel after the Holocaust, and WW2. The people stayed there until it was decided where to send them to live in Israel. My parents left after a few days because they knew through letters between them, that my father's brother lived in Nathanya, a city on the Mediterranean Sea.

Unfortunately, when they arrived in Nathanya, they discovered that Abraham had married and was now living in Zefat, (Safed, a city in the northern Galilee) so my parents and I went there to meet my uncle and to celebrate our first Passover in Israel together.

Later on, we came back to Nathanya.

It was a very difficult time and not at all peaceful. Palestine was under the rule of the British Mandate and the Jews wanted them to leave. Three parties, the Etzel, the Lechi and the Hagana fought to expel the British. My father joined the Lechi.

When I was about two and a half years old, my mother took me to Czechoslovakia to see if there was anyone left from her family after the war. My father couldn't come with us because he was involved in the conflict against the British.

My mother found one brother, Benjamin, who came to live in Israel because of her. All the rest of my mother's family had perished in the Holocaust; two sisters, Renée who was already married with a baby boy, Grete who was 17 years old and my grandparents, Menachem and Lea Bonitzer. All murdered.

My father also lost his family in the Holocaust: parents Yaacov and Rachel Zelmanovitch and a sister and a brother whose names sadly I do not know.

On 14th May 1948, after the War of Independence, the State of Israel was declared. There were no happier people around the whole wide world than we, the people of Israel!

After that time, my parents started to build their life in their new country, new language and a very different mentality.

My sister Lea, was born on 22nd of December 1947.

Eva (Zelmanovitch) Porcilan, daughter, 2021, Israel

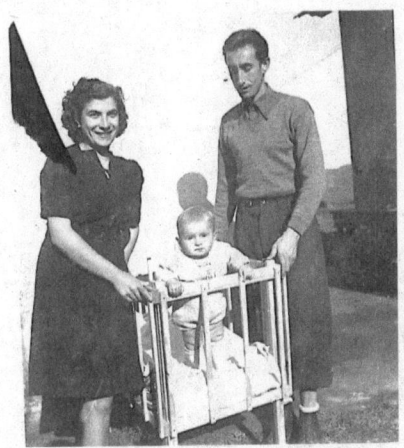

Sarah, Shlomo and Eva

Sarah with baby Eva

Sarah and Shlomo in Ferramonti

Ferramonti friends. Sarah, second right, front row.

Eva today

Adolfo (Foffo) Zippel

My father, Adolfo (Foffo) Zippel was born in Milan on January 6, 1916. He was the son of Jacob Meir Zippel, born in Zgierz (near Lodz) in Poland in July 1872. Jacob fled from there to Germany, encouraged by his father Avraham (born 1820), to avoid enlisting in the Russian-Polish war.

In Germany, he was welcomed by the local Rabbi, who taught him the practice and the laws of *Shechità* as well as providing a *Shidduch* with a girl of the German Jewish upper middle class. His Polish origins however were looked down upon by German aristocracy who used the term *Ostjuden* as a pejorative.

The Rabbi told him that they were looking for a *Shochet* in Turin, Italy, so around 1907 Jacob moved there to practice *Shechità* in the hope of consolidating a few Jewish practices among a population partially unaccustomed to strict Jewish tradition.

In Turin his wife Amalie (born Lewin, April 1885), gave birth to Herta, Carlo Shlomo Yosef, Harry Haim, Foffo Avrohom (my father), Hannah, Edi Gershom, and later in Germany, Ruth Sosha. After having practiced *Schechità* for the first years, having had access to the carcasses of many animals, he obtained an order from the Ministry of Defence to supply boots for the military: Italy was at war and invaded Russia. The business was profitable, but the level of Jewish observance was poor and this convinced him in 1922 to return to Wiesbaden, Germany, where he thought the family might benefit from a more observant Jewish community.

The Weimar Republic, reduced the family finances so drastically that they returned to Italy in 1933, this time to Milan, where the Jewish community was both more numerous and observant even if somewhat lukewarm.

Until 1938 things were fairly peaceful apart from one occasion, when my father's brother, Harry, going to the Piazza del Duomo to hear a speech by Mussolini, refused to raise his arm in salutation and got a beating. In 1938, the year in which grandmother Amalia died, the racial laws made things much more difficult. Uncle Edi Gershom was stopped on the tram one day and asked by the Fascists for his papers. He simply presented his railway ticket to avoid incriminating himself and when asked about his religion, replied, "That of Jesus."

My father, Adolfo (Foffo) Avrohom, was sent to *confino libero* by the Fascists in 1939, first to Terni then to Caserta, Salerno. He described it as a surprisingly pleasant period as his job was teaching basic literacy and numeracy to the adults of the village, mostly illiterate peasants. The women, who always took a shine to his good looks, paid him in loaves, cheese, eggs and other household goods for teaching their family members; he never suffered from hunger and was even able to share the benefits with others. If I remember rightly, he told us that retrospectively he felt lucky, having had the opportunity to take an occasional shower. Such *mazal* (luck) was uncommon.

He was then sent to Ferramonti di Tarsia in September 1941. There he made a friend, Avraham Sperber of German (Berlin) origin, whom he reconnected with later in Milan as a member of the synagogue my father founded in 1946.

According to his stories, life in Ferramonti passed uneventfully. My father was a handsome man, attractive, charismatic, with a deep and magnetic gaze; he had great success with the ladies.

In Ferramonti over the years people mostly died of natural causes. I remember that my father would talk about nearby villagers as being generally friendly towards the Jews, so much so that when one of the inmates died, the local priest agreed to enclose a small area of the cemetery to enable him to receive a Jewish burial. The Comandante Paolo Salvatore, always behaved with humanity and decency, repeatedly resisting Nazi instructions to send the Jews north (where they would have been dispatched to their deaths).

In July 1943, the Americans landed in Sicily, and my father decided it was time to escape, cross the lines and return to Milan to reunite with his family. Luckily he succeeded. Subsequently, the internment camp was liberated by the British.

The American landing in Sicily prompted Herta, my father's oldest sister, now mother of two children Carmi and Reha, to come to Italy from Israel, in search of her parents and brothers, thinking that the war would soon be over. But things took a turn for the worse because on 13 September 1943 the Nazis officially settled in Milan at the Hotel Regina. All the Jews, those on the run or hiding in the countryside, now faced a terrible fate. Jacob Zippel and his sons made a plan to flee to Switzerland, but a large family would have attracted attention, even crossing hills and passes at night, so they split into 3 groups. Two groups managed to cross the border thanks to paid smugglers, but the third group—that of their sister Herta, with her husband Isaac, and their children Carmi and Reha - was betrayed by the Swiss border guards who sent them back to Italy where they were incarcerated in Varese. From there they were sent to San Vittore prison in Milan and after two weeks of suffering, loaded on a cattle wagon and sent to die in Auschwitz on 7 August 1944, recognized by a surviving family friend, who saw them entering the gas showers. She wrote a book about the events, "Il Silenzio dei Vivi," by Elisa Springer.

Life in the Swiss internment camp at Raron was harsh. There were many restrictions, very few visits were allowed and hardly any exit permits granted. Grandfather Jacob was not even allowed to buy medicine for his cancer pains. According to my father the notorious Swiss "courtesy" and hypocrisy, was never lost on the inmates.

My father married my mother, Meta Maline Weil (a Swiss citizen, born February 21, 1918) on June 30th, 1946. They returned to Milan together with his brothers Harry and Edi while sisters Hanna and Ruth married Eisiq Ornstein and Jack Lunzer, and lived in Zurich and London respectively.

In 1946, my father, after regularly hosting the daily minyan at home with growing numbers of Holocaust survivors, established the Ohel Jaakov Congregation on 9th June, in the rented premises in Via Cellini 2, Milan. This address became famous in the post-war period among all those Jews of Ashkenazi origin, whether living there or just passing through, who wanted to recreate and relive the traditions of the lost world that Nazism had destroyed in Europe. Incidentally, since then in the Shul of Via Cellini, the tefillot are celebrated 3 times a day and for many years in Milan it was the only synagogue where you could recite *tefillot* daily and recite the *Kaddish* with a *minyan*. Shabbat services in the 1960s were attended by more than 60 families. Today it's a bit more difficult but the minyan is organized with the help of social media.

In those years, my father and his brothers went into the wholesale fur business eventually opening 6 branches of their company in Italy, ultimately moving into the manufacture of fur garments.

In 1956 they were joined by their brother Carlo, who had previously taken refuge in England, upon the recommendation of Astorre Meier, another benefactor of Jewish Milan. Having had contact with the Lubavitcher Rebbe Menahem Mendel Schneerson, in 1956, Carlo with my father, Harry and Edi welcomed the first *Shaliach* of the Rebbe in Europe: Rav Gershon Mendel Garelik who became the forerunner of Chabad activities in Italy. Then in Milan, Rav Berl Lazar, was born to Rav Moshe Lazar my Bar Mitzvah tutor, that same Berl Lazar who became Head of the Rabbinate of Russia and a personal friend of Vladimir Putin. The chief Rabbi of Budapest, Rav Baruch Oberlander is also linked to Milan, being married to Batsheva Rachel Oberlander Lazar. In the 1960s, my father and uncles financed the organization of summer camps, Ganei Israel near Lake Como, and established a *Chabad* school in premises of theirs, with secular and Jewish subjects for children, up to middle school, with an attendance at that time of about 150 children, nowadays over two hundred. Permission was also granted for the construction of a kosher *Mikveh* using the cellars of the premises.

My father passed away on August 7, 1977 at the age of 61, after a long illness caused by lung cancer, leaving our widowed mother with her children Daniela Zippel in Mevorah, Vera Zippel in Rosen and myself Giacomo Michele Zippel born in 1950.

Giacomo Michele (Jacky) Zippel, Jerusalem

Grandfather Jacob Zippel

Herta with husband Isaac and children Carmi and Reha. All perished in Auschwitz.

My parents Meta and Foffo Zippel

My parents with me and my sisters, 1950s

www.ingramcontent.com/pod-product-compliance
Lightning Source LLC
LaVergne TN
LVHW032202070526
838202LV00008B/284